W9-DGR-597

Date Due

Ludwig Lewisohn

Twayne's United States Authors Series

Kenneth Eble, Editor

University of Utah

TUSAS 435

LUDWIG LEWISOHN
(1883-1955)
Photograph courtesy
of Brandeis University

Ludwig Lewisohn

By Seymour Lainoff

Yeshiva University

Twayne Publishers • Boston

Ludwig Lewisohn

Seymour Lainoff
Copyright © 1982 by G. K. Hall & Company
All Rights Reserved
Published by Twayne Publishers
A Division of G. K. Hall & Company
70 Lincoln Street
Boston, Massachusetts 02111

Book Production by Marne B. Sultz
Book Design by Barbara Anderson

Printed on permanent/durable acid-
free paper and bound in The United
States of America.

Library of Congress Cataloging in Publication Data

Lainoff, Seymour.
Ludwig Lewisohn.

(Twayne's United States authors series;
TUSAS 435)
   Bibliography: p. 139
   Includes index.
   1. Lewisohn, Ludwig, 1883-1955
—Criticism and interpretation.
I. Title. II. Series.
PS3523.E96Z59   1982   813'.52   82-11791
ISBN 0-8057-7375-4

Contents

About the Author

Seymour Lainoff is Professor of English Literature at Yeshiva University. He has also taught at The City College of New York and Hofstra University. He received his B. A. degree at Brooklyn College, his M. A. at Columbia University, and his Ph. D. at New York University. Professor Lainoff has participated in panel discussions on American literature on television, both on WNBC and WNYC, and has been awarded a National Foundation of Jewish Culture grant and a New York State War Veterans Regents Fellowship. He has published numerous articles and reviews, including studies on Henry James, Stephen Crane, Shirley Jackson, and American fiction, in *Modern Fiction Studies, College English, Nineteenth Century Fiction, Studies in English Literature, Criticism, Symposium, Explicator,* and other journals. He co-edited (with Dr. Sidney D. Braun) *Transatlantic Mirrors: Essays in Franco-American Literary Relations,* Twayne, 1978.

Preface

In the 1920s, especially, and in the 1930s, Ludwig Lewisohn (1883–1955), novelist, critic, and polemicist, was considered a figure of some significance in American literature. Now—except in Jewish circles—he is almost forgotten. This decline in reputation needs redress, for, among the forty volumes he composed over half a century, at least five have distinctive and permanent merit.

True, much of his work has deservedly fallen into the limbo where, as Dryden states in *MacFlecknoe:* "No Persian carpets spread th'imperial way/ But scatter'd limbs of mangled poets lay/..." But the writing of five good books remains no mean feat. These are, roughly in order of merit: *The Case of Mr. Crump* (1926), a fine Naturalistic novel, a riveting and pitiless portrait of marital discord, one of the best American novels in a rich decade of American fiction; *The Island Within* (1928), a superior thesis novel, written with wit and irony; *Up Stream* (1923), one of the best autobiographies of the period, possessing dramatic focus and organization; *Cities and Men* (1927), bearing some of the best of his voluminous criticism, capping a decade of good critical writing; *Israel* (1925), a vivid book of travel and polemics, farsighted in its view of international drifts in the 1920s. These, at least, cannot be disregarded by those interested in American letters. One might mention as well *Expression in America* (1932), a literary history of the United States, the better passages of which are matched by equally poor ones. His best work was done in one decade of a long career.

This decline in reputation can be partially attributed to the publicity—to which Lewisohn contributed in his fiction and especially in his later two autobiographies—given to his matrimonial entanglements and also, as he himself stated, to his later fervent advocacy of Judaism and Zionism. A stigma of sorts has attached itself to him. As late as 1971, Leslie A. Fiedler saw him as a ludicruous figure, a pathetic display of the Jew suffering contortions in the unaccustomed role of Don Juan.[1] Fiedler, too, thought his later Zionism an escape from literature. In his assessment, Fiedler was following a tradition, beginning in the 1920s, which saw Lewisohn as a "case," a tradition which arose even in the time of Lewisohn's greatest fame and which somehow has outlived that fame.

Certainly, nobody found anything to object to before *Up Stream*; Lewisohn was then known mainly for his valuable and objective criticism and scholarship. Before and during the First World War Lewisohn did commendable academic work introducing German and other Continental authors to American readers; he displayed a breadth of knowledge of other modern literatures uncommon in the United States. In his years (1919–1924) with the *Nation* he produced first-rate drama criticism, conscientious, exact, and just.

But, in his sojourn or exile in Europe during the next decade, he wrote a different kind of literature—novels, criticism, and autobiography with subjective roots. Literature, he often wrote, was a form of autobiography, and, even though the products of this decade include much of his best work, his life and writings now seemed to many both unusual and perplexing. Three articles about him were entitled "The Case of Mr. Lewisohn," attesting to what seemed an ostensible neurosis or psychosis. As James Waterman Wise wrote in 1928, "His intellectual growth, his sex experience, his emotional development, his spiritual adventures, are alike set down for all men to read and know. One might even...gather his writings under one comprehensive title: The Case of Ludwig Lewisohn."[2] Many reviewers and critics felt uneasy with this unexpected exhibition of passion.

At the same time Lewisohn became gradually more Jewish-minded, this interest displacing, often though never entirely, the universal literary standards of his criticism. His marital embroilments, the subject of gossip and attack, hurt his image and prompted him at times to adopt postures of self-pity and self-justification. His growing religiosity and continued marital difficulties presented a paradox difficult to understand.

His literary talents conceded, different views of "The Case of Ludwig Lewisohn" circulated. James W. Wise thought his turn to subjectivity wholesome since it coincided with an eloquent advocacy of Jewish tenets. David Eckerling, in 1929, admired the earlier objective critic but thought the later, more subjective, more aggressive Lewisohn overly personal and unpleasantly combative.[3] (Eckerling wrote his article after the publication of *Mid-Channel,* one of Lewisohn's most contentious works.) The first sentence in Louis J. Bragman's "The Case of Ludwig Lewisohn," in the *American Journal of Psychiatry,* stated that Lewisohn suffered from "disturbed germ plasm"! Bragman, a physician turned critic, was commendatory and insightful, but helped fix the impression that Lewisohn, however talented, was a neurotic.[4]

It is time, at last, to put aside Lewisohn as a "case" and see him as a writer. In reading the whole body of his work, one uncovers a store of good writing that has been relatively neglected. Today, in our more permissive times, Lewisohn's personal difficulties stir much less nonliterary interest, and when such difficulties are rendered the subject of fiction, as in Bellow's *Herzog* (1964) or I. B. Singer's *Shosha* (1978), Lewisohn's works can be read and examined with greater detachment.

Milton Hindus, a colleague of Lewisohn's at Brandeis University in Lewisohn's last years, in an appreciation of the author written in 1964—some years after his death—has recognized his solid merits beyond the agony-ridden picture drawn by some of his contemporaries.[5] Hindus cites his mastery of English style, "such as none of his co-religionists in his generation had yet achieved"; the appreciation extended him by Henry L. Mencken, Thomas Mann, Freud, and others of note; the excellence of his oratory, his spellbinding quality as speaker. Similarly, I wish to emphasize the trained scholar, the independent man of letters, the author of at least two significant novels, the master of several genres of writing, rather than the tortured egoist others have seen.

In this enterprise I was assisted by a summer grant from Yeshiva University and a grant for 1979–1980 from the Memo-

LUDWIG LEWISOHN

rial Foundation for Jewish Culture. I wish to express my appreciation as well for helpful hints to Dr. Sidney Braun, Dr. Maurice Wohlgernter, and Dr. Abraham L. Sachar, retired Chancellor of Brandeis University, and to the libraries of Yeshiva, Columbia, and Brandeis Universities, the last of which allowed me to examine its Lewisohn archives. My greatest appreciation is extended to my wife, Lila, whose patience during this writing was exemplary.

Seymour Lainoff

Yeshiva University

Chronology

1883   Ludwig Lewisohn born on May 30, in Berlin, the only child of Jacques and Minna Lewisohn.

1890   Family emigrated to South Carolina; two years later they moved to Charleston.

1893   Admitted to the High School of Charleston.

1897   Entered the College of Charleston.

1901   Received B. A. and M. A. degrees in English literature simultaneously.

1903   Began graduate study at Columbia University, but did not complete his doctoral studies, discouraged by evidences of anti-Semitism standing in the way of his securing a university teaching position.

1906   Married Mary Arnold Child Crocker, twenty years his senior; unhappy marriage not formally dissolved until 1937. Earned a livelihood through literary hackwork.

1908   First novel, *The Broken Snare.*

1910   Secured an instructorship in German at the University of Wisconsin; the next year transferred to Ohio State University. Wrote critical studies of German and Continental literature from 1912 to 1917; in 1917 felt forced to leave Ohio State because of manifestations of hostility toward his pacifist and neutralist sentiments during the War.

1919–1924   Assumed drama desk at the *Nation.* Collections of reviews and articles appeared in book form.

1922   *Up Stream*, first and best of his autobiographies, published.

1924   Still married to Mary Crocker, ran off with Thelma Spear, a young singer, to Europe, where they maintained residence for a decade.

1926   *The Case of Mr. Crump*, an autobiographical novel, privately published in Paris; first published in the United States in 1947.

1928   *The Island Within*, his best novel of Jewish content.

1932   *Expression in America*, a history of American literature.

1933   His only child, James Elias Lewisohn, born of Thelma Spear, on September 17.

1940   Marriage to Edna Manley, not long after breakup with Thelma Spear; contested custody of son in the courts, the mother receiving custody in 1941.

1940–1948   Assumed column in and, in 1943, editorship of the *New Palestine*, evidencing his strong involvement with Zionism.

1944   Marriage to Miss Louise Wolk after divorce from Edna Manley Lewisohn.

1948   Appointed Professor of Comparative Literature at Brandeis University and, in 1955, University Librarian.

1955   Died of a heart attack in Miami on December 31.

Chapter One
Mainly Autobiography
Queenshaven: The Making of an American

The title of Ludwig Lewisohn's *Up Stream* (1922)—the first of his three autobiographical volumes and the best—suggests a salmon swimming upstream, against the current, to discover his breeding grounds. One arrives at this analogy because of Lewisohn's attempt at complete assimilation into the mainstream of American life and his return to his Jewish origins, a *volte face* that proved the central event in Lewisohn's life and work. Since Lewisohn, many American Jews, moved by the Holocaust and the ordeals of the state of Israel, have been led to a "return to ethnicity."

Yet *Up Stream* concludes, unlike some of Lewisohn's later works, only with a faint acknowledgment of Judaism; more pressingly it raises a battle cry against "Puritanism," the timid conventionalism of the American scene, and the genteel tradition in American letters. Lewisohn's first rebellion, confirmed later by his reading of Freud, was shared by many of his generation. He engaged in the protest which attracted such diverse other figures as James Huneker, H. L. Mencken, Van Wyck Brooks, and Sinclair Lewis. Lewisohn proceeded first from a complete acquiescence to the ideals of his Southern upbringing to a literary and sexual rebellion, and only later, as merely foreshadowed in *Up Stream*, to a sense of Jewish identification. This last position was, to an extent, both a reversal of his first rebellion and an outgrowth of it.

He was born on May 30, 1883,[1] in Berlin, the only child of Jacques and Minna Eleosser Lewisohn, who were first cousins. Though he was taken to America at age seven, the man later remembered the Berlin of his childhood vividly and found his impressions, in a later visit to the city in the 1920s, to be accurate.

He was to recall that his family lived in comfortable circumstances. His forbears had lived in Germany for generations and were assimilated, thinking of themselves as Germans first and Jews second. He writes that his "grandfather had much rabbinical learning, but a whimsical contempt for the ritual law...."[2] An uncle had won the Iron Cross. The boy Ludwig had a Christmas tree. His father, a cultivated reader, was strongly influenced by Haeckel and other post-Darwinian naturalists. His father's financial ruin led the family to emigrate in 1890 to the United States, settling in St. Matthews ("St. Marks") in South Carolina, a new community of two central streets, with twelve Jewish families from whom the Lewisohns were estranged. His father, Louis J. Bragman—a psychiatrist turned critic—writes, was "a dreamer and a quasi-inventor, developing a brooding melancholy, with weird and eccentric traits...."[3] Two years later they moved to Charleston, slightly disguised as "Queenshaven" in *Up Stream*.

There the Lewisohn family practiced no Jewish observances, but the young Lewisohn received a religious training. His parents sent him to Sunday school in the Methodist Church. He seems to have had, more than his father, a religious bent at this early age: "I accepted Jesus as my personal Savior and cultivated, with vivid faith, the habit of prayer in which I persisted for many years" (*Up*, 53). He writes further: "...at the age of fifteen I was an American, a Southerner, and a Christian" (*Up*, 85).

In his bookish childhood his first favorites were Sir Walter Scott and Dickens. This love of reading was strengthened during his attendance at the High School of Charleston ("Queenshaven"), to which he was admitted in October 1893. The school provided a good literary and linguistic training. He did not take Greek, an elective study, an omission he later called an "irreparable loss"; but he laid the foundation of his later knowledge of Latin and French, which supplemented his native fluency in German. For a whole year his chief pleasure was Macaulay, who led him to Milton, Dryden, and eighteenth-century English literature. At thirteen he began writing verses and hoped one day to be a poet; his parents, especially his mother, encouraged his literary aspirations. In his last year of high school he rendered his own translations of Horace. There, too, he must have developed the work and study habits that were to make him later so assiduous a literary practitioner.

Falling in with a group of boys who belonged to the gentle families of the city, he adapted to a refined and Christian Southern environment. Unlike his friends, however, he did not enjoy "games," or sports. He was troubled, too, with thoughts of sex, which fed his sense of guilt and sin, partly instilled by his Methodist training. He writes also: "I was the more convinced of the wickedness of my thoughts by the absurd exaltation of woman which is so characteristic a note of Southern life" (*Up*, 81). Later, as novelist and essayist, he was to protest against the tradition of sexual repression in which he had been reared.

The College of Charleston ("Queenshaven"), which he entered upon graduation from high school in 1897, helped him bury disturbing thoughts of sex. It was a "place of peace—gentle, with an eighteenth-century repose." Here, stirred by his love of English literature, he decided to complement his future literary career with an academic one: he would become a college professor of English. He spent much time during those four years with a teacher who held a chair in English, "Ferris" (Lancelot Minor Harris). "Ferris," a Virginian, was talented, his student thought, but too much the gentleman to be an artist. He shared with Lewisohn a love of England and English letters. But the younger man always felt in his mentor a shade of withdrawal. Lewisohn, reading much in nineteenth-century prose, was moved by Walter Pater, Robert Louis Stevenson, and especially Matthew Arnold, who taught him the importance of culture and criticism in society and, at a later time, the general need for both Hebraism and Hellenism. From these writers and from a Southern tradition of oratory Lewisohn was to derive his sometimes rhetorical, sometimes florid, prose style. The verse he wrote at this time Lewisohn dismisses as worthless—derivative, without direct vision. (Though Lewisohn continued to write verse for most of his life, his poetry remained derivative and helplessly Victorian.)

His college years seemed happy, though somewhat subdued. He remained a Christian: "I still, during these years, attended the

Methodist Church, taught Sunday school, and was a leader in the Epsworth League" (*Up*, 99). But, in this smooth flow, he suffered two setbacks. In his senior year he was excluded from a fraternity formed of his classmates, friends, and even admirers. He felt ostracized. Also, in his last two years, he fell in love, and would have married the girl since physical love was otherwise forbidden. The relationship came to an end.

After his commencement in 1901, at which time he received two degrees, those of Bachelor and Master of Arts, he was, because of his academic achievements, something of a local hero. (He was to secure an honorary doctorate from the College of Charleston in 1914.) Extracts from his master's thesis on Matthew Arnold appeared in the *Sewanee Review* in 1901 and 1902. But he did not win a scholarship or fellowship to Columbia or Harvard, though both were willing to admit him into their graduate schools. A year later a group of "Queenshaven" gentlemen presented him with $350 for graduate studies at Columbia. As he left the South, he remained, despite omens in his college years, passionately Anglo-American in his sympathies. He wanted, above all, though his name and appearance were characteristically Jewish, to be an Anglo-American man of letters. He wrote and had published, in the Sunday editions of the *Charleston News-and-Courier* from July 5 to September 20, 1903, a 50,000-word essay on the literature of South Carolina from its beginnings to the Civil War.[4] His point of view was Southern.

Lewisohn on Arnold

Lewisohn's three articles on Matthew Arnold in the *Sewanee Review* (October 1901, April 1902, July 1902)—on Arnold's poetry, on those who influenced him, and on his critical method, respectively—deserve at least brief mention, not only for their considerable intrinsic value, but also because they mark a transition in Lewisohn's development from his adolescent Christianity to his espousal of Naturalism in his twenties.

Lewisohn takes issue with George Saintsbury's designation of Arnold's poetry as a blending of "Wordsworthian enthusiasm and Byronic despair." First, Arnold's view of nature differs from Wordsworth's. The earlier poet loved nature, in his own words, as "the living garment of the Deity"; in contrast, Lewisohn writes, "Arnold's view of nature is the view of modern science, Nature is calm, restful, cruel, but just." Arnold lived in an aftermath of Christianity, with a deep regret that he had lost his father's faith. Second, Byron's despair was of one sated with earthly enjoyment. On the other hand, Lewisohn continues, "the despair of Arnold was the despair of the intellect, which saw the ancient faith of the world passing away, and found nothing to replace it." Though Arnold abandoned his Christian faith, he never forgot the impressions of childhood, living in the *nachschein* of his training.

Another subject of Arnold's poetry, which later led him to forsake poetry for a prose with a preaching intent, was the philistinism of modern life: in Lewisohn's phrasing, "the blindness of men, their hard materialized lives, the necessity of seeking help at the inner shrine of the soul." To deal with the shortcomings of the modern age, Arnold sought refuge particularly in Goethe, who led Arnold to seek classical restraint and a striving for inner perfection.

Reading these surprisingly mature essays by the twenty-year-old Lewisohn, one feels his identification with Arnold. Lewisohn, too, has strayed from his early religiosity with regret; in German Naturalism he will find evidence of a true picture of nature; and he will later do battle with the Philistines and Puritans on the American scene.

Graduate School: Disillusionment

The second half of *Up Stream*, less incisive than the first, tends to gloss over facts and editorialize more. Though the reader finds it harder to piece together the events of his life, it is easy enough to see that Lewisohn's graduate-school years were unhappy and disillusioning. The Columbia experience, accompanied by penury and loneliness, produced a sense of failure rather than fulfillment. He found at the Graduate School a paucity of ideas; professors ladled out information he already possessed: "In a word, I was an ardent disciple and I found no master." Lewisohn possibly plays down the continued kindness shown him by William P. Trent (the "Brent" of *Up Stream*), Chairman of the Graduate English Department, who shared with Lewisohn the enterprise of editing Crévecoeur's *Letters from an American Farmer* (New York: Fox Duffield, 1904)—an unusual privilege for a graduate student, then as now. For this edition, still useful, Lewisohn wrote an extended introduction.

While attending graduate school, he began on his own to read extensively in modern German literature, from Nietzsche to Rilke. This literature, for him, incorporated a veracity and a flexibility in its views of human nature that he found lacking in English literature. The latter, he states, except for the eighteenth century, remained remote from life. The central weakness of the Anglo-American mind, in his diagnosis, was its false idealism, its "moral illusionism." Modern German writers, on the other hand, "made me free; they set me on the road of trying to be not what was thought correct without reference to reality, but what I was naturally meant to be" (*Up*, 133). His interest in modern German literature with its realistic tenor probably reflected his own coping at this time with the need for self-support, the promptings of sex, and living in New York, a city which seemed "brutal, ferocious, stark." Revealing, too, perhaps, a measure of homesickness, Lewisohn cultivated acquaintances in the German community of New York, including the Vierecks. An article by Lewisohn in the *Sewanee Review* in 1904 also appeared as a prefatory appreciation to George Sylvester Viereck's limited edition of poems, *Gedichte* (1904).

German literature thus proved a consolation and a guide. A second source of encouragement was the friendship of the poet "Ellard" (William Ellery Leonard), whom he met at Columbia. But obstacles presented themselves. After receiving his master's degree, his second one, at the end of his first year, in 1903, during which time he earned his way by tutoring, he was not elected, despite very high grades, to a scholarship or fellowship. Furthermore, he could get no teaching appointment because he was a

Jew—a real barrier then if not now. His friends at Columbia were called into conference with Professor "Brewer" (George Rice Carpenter), the Secretary of the Department, to discuss teaching appointments; he was not. In response to a letter he sent "Brewer" about a possible teaching job, he received this chilling reply, which Lewisohn records verbatim:

It is very sensible of you to look so carefully into your plans and at this juncture, because I do not at all believe in the wisdom of your scheme. A recent experience has shown me how terribly hard it is for a man of Jewish birth to get a good position. I had always suspected that it was a matter worth considering, but I had not known how widespread and strong it was. While we shall be glad to do anything we can for you, therefore, I cannot help feeling that the chances are going to be greatly against you. (*Up*, 142–43)

The letter, which proves the climax to *Up Stream,* crushed Lewisohn. It added anti-Semitism, which he had not consciously permitted to touch him before, to the feelings of inadequacy he had developed as an outsider in Charleston, who had compensated by academic overachievement, and as one encountering the problems of young manhood in New York. The structure of success he had envisioned for his life had collapsed. Adolph Gillis wrote in 1933: "To this day Professor Trent recalls Lewisohn's disheveled appearance during these months of anxiety...the revealing unbalance of despair."[5]

Lewisohn announced his abandoning the pursuit of his doctorate, despite Trent's protests. He apparently had written drafts of his dissertation, but felt too discouraged to continue. He felt an iron prejudice that was useless to combat. His dream of becoming an Anglo-American scholar was shattered. The destiny that awaited him, as it turned out, was more complex.

Already struggling to achieve selfhood, he felt, upon receiving "Brewer's" letter, that he was an outcast. Such was his introduction to Judaism. He writes in *Up Stream*: "... for the first time in my life my heart turned with grief and remorse to the thoughts of my brethren in exile all over the world..." (*Up*, 144). But in 1904 and 1905, years before the writing of *Up Stream*, this sense of identity with other Jews must have been a faint glimmer.

A Literary Career Commences

The four years after Lewisohn left Columbia provided no rest in what proved to be a troubled and controversial life and career. After working briefly at Warner's Library, Lewisohn secured a position as reader, with Trent's assistance, with the New York publishers Doubleday, Page and Company. He regarded his work there as drudgery and his fellow employees as "slaves in soul." For two years he engaged in this apparently degrading work and in free-lance writing.

In 1906 he married Mary Arnold Child Crocker, an English-born, non-Jewish divorced woman, who, in her subsequent career as minor poet and playwright, assumed the penname of Bos-worth Crocker. Born on March 2, 1863, twenty years Lewisohn's senior, she had four grown children and was a grandmother. This unhappy marriage, the first of Lewisohn's complicated marital entanglements, was not dissolved in New York until 1937. This seeming misalliance was the source of his second novel, *Don Juan* (1923), and of his most powerful novel, *The Case of Mr. Crump* (1926), which treat in fiction his own tortured experience. His attention was turned permanently to the difficulties of love and marriage as chief subject for his fiction. In *Up Stream* his references to his first wife are few and reticent, including one, affectionate in tone, to "the bright hair and grey English eyes of my own wife...."

Lewisohn began composing fiction, he writes, essentially to supplement his income as a struggling young married man. After studying the structure of the short story by reading tales by Henry James, he wrote three stories for *Smart Set*, all of which had first been rejected by the *Atlantic Monthly*; he wrote a fourth story for the *Uncle Remus* magazine in Atlanta and then more stories for *Smart Set*. In 1907 and 1908 he also wrote for *Town Topics*, a New York weekly. Quitting his job with the publishing firm and desperate for funds, he wrote six potboiling serials in a row, an effort which left him in a state of self-disgust.

To maintain his integrity, he wrote a serious novel, published in 1908 as *The Broken Snare*. Theodore Dreiser, who read it for B. W. Dodge and Company, recommended it for publication. The book, which Lewisohn called "naturalistic," dealt with a love relationship outside of marriage. Though well-received by reviewers, the novel had no luck with the general public and even met with some obloquy. (Today, of course, the novel seems mild.) The *Charleston News-and-Courier*, Lewisohn's early literary outlet, called it "a profoundly disgusting story."[6] The plates for his next novel, Lewisohn states, were seized by Anthony Comstock, a leading figure before World War I in the reactionary fight against a greater freedom in literary expression, and destroyed. No wonder Lewisohn was to attack "Puritanism" and "provincialism," terms which became shibboleths in his later writings. In *Up Stream* Lewisohn describes himself at this point as follows: "I was beaten, broken, breadless. I was a scholar and forbidden to teach, an artist and forbidden to write. Liberty, opportunity, the words had nothing friendly to my ears" (*Up*, 171).

A Professorship in German and the War Years

Seeking a means of livelihood after his practical failure as a novelist, Lewisohn had no recourse but to seek help from Professor "Brent" (Trent) at Columbia. Vacancies in English existed at the Universities of Virginia, Michigan, Minnesota, and Wisconsin, but these departments rejected him. Lewisohn states without hesitation that he was turned down at these places because he was Jewish; undoubtedly, he was better qualified than the average candidate. Finally, through the intervention of his friend, the poet William Ellery Leonard, then teaching English at Wisconsin, Lewisohn was offered, in 1910, an instructorship in German at that University. Though Lewisohn accepted the post, he always considered teaching German an entrance into college teaching through the back door. Before assuming his task, Lewisohn, as always undertaking wholeheartedly his responsibilities, edited a small volume, *German Style* (1910), an anthology and historical survey with some critical apparatus.

After one year at Wisconsin, he left to teach German at Ohio State University at Columbus, where he was to remain for six years. With the change he received a raise in salary and an assistant professorship. In addition to teaching, he commenced yeoman service as a literary intermediary between Europe, especially Germany, and the United States, in the tradition of Percival Pollard and James Huneker: editing, translating, and interpreting for American readers. His authorized edition and translations of the plays of Gerhart Hauptmann (running to seven volumes from 1912 to 1915) were standard for decades. He also translated at this time works by Hermann Sudermann and Georg Hirschfeld, as he was later to translate Jacob Wasserman, Franz Werfel, Soma Morgenstern, and Jacob Picard. His books *Modern Drama* (1915), *The Spirit of Modern German Literature* (1916), and *The Poets of Modern France* (1918) did much to acquaint Americans with recent Continental letters.

Lewisohn was at this time an enthusiastic Germanist, in the cultural and artistic spheres. In his 1916 introduction to his translation of Georg Hirschfeld's *The Mothers*, he writes: "The characteristic modes of thought and feeling of the North German and those of the Jew who has discarded his archaic Orientalism are profoundly alike. Both have the same earnestness in the conduct of life, the same strong family sense, the hard practical intelligence—the capacity, too, of producing now and then individuals of the finest sensitiveness and power...."[7]

The passage indicates that his identification with Judaism at this time was no stronger, and probably weaker, than his identification with certain German modes and ideals. Lewisohn writes that he was an advocate of "modern German literature and civilization as embodying the widest moral and intellectual liberty and tireless spiritual stirring."[8] (These quotations mark a sharp contrast to the second chapter of *Israel* (1925), in which Lewisohn not only saw the rising tide of anti-Semitism in Germany but also the unwillingness of the German Jewish intellectual community to recognize this threat.)

Lewisohn stressed idealism and moral freedom in his classes and writings; toward the end of *Up Stream*, Lewisohn excoriates the philistinism, materialism, and spiritual emptiness of the American Midwest, as exemplified by "Central City" (Columbus, Ohio). The University itself, he argues, merely reflected the greater environment instead of affecting it for the better: "The hardwareman and the undertaker have triumphed." Despite his opposition to the conformities dominating the campus and city, Lewisohn claims he evoked much loyalty and affection among his students—though he was "frankly merciless to the popular fallacies and the mass delusions amid which they had to live." Lewisohn takes the occasion, also, to attack the censorship exerted against authors during the pre-War period. In words akin to John Stuart Mill's *On Liberty*, but owing more, probably, to Nietzsche, Lewisohn writes: "When the personal consciousness emerges from the merely tribal consciousness—this is the birth of liberty" (*Up*, 234). His position marks a turn away from his earlier conformism; it also is at variance with his later Judaic posture.

The section of *Up Stream* devoted to his professorship at Ohio State takes on the coloration of a battle fought "as on a darkling plain." The death of his mother 1912 and of his father in 1917 added to his growing somberness of mood. Finally, as the Great War began, Lewisohn was harassed by the mounting anti-German hysteria of the period. When Lewisohn, who asserted a love of German culture and a pacifism in international affairs, published his nonpolitical *Spirit of Modern German Literature* in 1916, he was attacked by figures in the Columbus community; he even suffered a moderate dressing-down by the president of the University. In 1917, taking a year's leave of absence, Lewisohn left Ohio State, never to return.

Chapter 10 of *Up Stream* attacks the "barbarism" of the war years and the war itself: "The great capitalistic groups who control industrial populations had come to blows over coal and oil and troopical estates and trade-routes. The Western group won and proceeded to ruin its great competitor" (*Up*, 276). To Lewisohn's credit, he not only consistently attacked the war and capitalism in its imperialistic phases, but also remained a resolute opponent of both Fascism and Communism; the last he saw, in the twenties and thirties, as another form of moral absolutism.

But his most persistent barrage in *Up Stream* is directed against attempts to make the American scene a single unvarying entity, a place of complete conformity. He argues the need for cultural pluralism and the preservation of older cultures: "The friend of the Republic, the lover of those values which alone make life endurable, must bid the German and the Jew, the Latin and the Slav preserve his cultural traditions..." (*Up*, 289-90). With the conclusion of the war, *Up Stream* ends, having recorded a young manhood filled more with anguish than triumph.

Up Stream: in Retrospect

In this review of Lewisohn's life up to World War I, I have relied chiefly on *Up Stream*, supplemented by some factual material from secondary sources. *Up Stream* remains, despite its occasional excesses of polemicism and self-dustification, one of the best autobiographies of its decade. Oscar Cargill wrote of it:

... undeniably an important book, both a moving human document and a fearless tract for racial equality. One is stirred to indignation that a man must suffer so much humiliation and injustice as is painfully set down in *Up Stream* merely because his blood is not that of the dominant stock in America. One does not believe, of course, that Lewisohn was always so descriminated against as he thinks he was.... And the record of national hostility during the war-hysteria to all things German— even in our universities—is mortifying.... *Up Stream* is the perfect antidote, with its broad cosmopolitan reference and its passion for universal culture, for 100% Americanism.[9]

Carl Van Doren in *Three Worlds* (1936) expressed sentiments similar to Cargill's about the autobiography.[10] Many critics and reviewers contemporary to Lewisohn received *Up Stream* favorably. H. L. Mencken wrote: "Few better autobiographies than his 'Upstream' have been done in America in our time."[11] Joseph Warren Beach, in 1926, declared the book "a very serious arraignment of race prejudice and of Puritanism, of an indubitable sincerity and power."[12]

Several critics were not so kind, condemning Lewisohn as the product of a "Teutonic" background. The *New York Times* gave the book to review to Brander Matthews, professor of dramatic literature at Columbia, whom Lewisohn had taken issue with in print; Matthews complained of what he took to be Lewisohn's arrogance, the outgrowth of his "Teutonic" proclivities.[13] (In response to Matthews, Anzia Yezierska, an intelligent and self-educated immigrant writer of fiction, wrote a spirited defense of the work, in the *Times*, April 23, 1922.)[14] Stuart Pratt Sherman commented harshly on *Up Stream*: "...Mr. Lewisohn drops the mask and reveals himself, for all his Jewish radicalism, as essentially a sentimental and homesick German, longing in exile for a Germany which exists only in his imagination."[15]

Stuart Pratt Sherman took a strong Humanist stand against the new rebellious critics, including Van Wyck Brooks and Mencken as well as Lewisohn. A disciple of More and Babbitt, but more nationalistic, Sherman believed that the newer critics sought inspiration too much from foreign sources, ignoring the tradition of independence found in Emerson, Thoreau, Whitman, and even the much-abused "Puritans." Sherman's position had some validity, but his strictures on Lewsohn seem excessive. Burton Rascoe, in his memoir *Before I Forget* (1937), wrote of Sherman's review in the *Nation* in 1917 of Mencken's *Book of Prefaces*: "The review was also anti-Semitic to a high degree, linking the Jews with Germans as inimical to the American tradition."[16] This intemperance carried over to Sherman's review of *Up Stream*.

A more temperate and reasonable opposition was voiced by Jacob Zeitlin, writing in the *Menorah Journal*. Professor Zeitlin, then at the University of Illinois, was later Sherman's biographer. Zeitlin finds the sources of Lewisohn's unhappiness not in anti-Semitism but in his spiritual "organization";

Lewisohn, he states, as a "sensitive, dreamy idealist," exaggerated the rigors of anti-Semitism in universities and American life. Zeitlin concludes of *Up Stream*: "As a document of its writer's mind, as a touching record of the sufferings of a sensitive spirit in adverse surroundings, its interest is of a high order... But his being a Jew seems only to be an accident in the story."[17]

Zeitlin, also a Jewish graduate student at Columbia, had received the same counsel, a short time after Lewisohn, from "Brester," discouraging him from continuing in academic life. But Zeitlin apparently chose to set this advice aside and succeeded in gaining a foothold. To Zeitlin, Lewisohn's problem was more a personal one than a general one.

To a degree, of course, Zeitlin was right in emphasizing Lewisohn's "spiritual organization" as the source of his woes. But one cannot deny the prejudice that Lewisohn detected and applied to himself. Though exceptions, such as Zeitlin, might be cited, being Jewish was a formidable barrier for teaching college English. Writing about a period two decades after Lewisohn's experience, Lionel Trilling discussed the hardship. His friend Elliot Cohen (later, for many years editor of *Commentary* magazine) "had given up the graduate study of English because he believed that as a Jew he had no hope of a university appointment. When I decided to go into academic life, my friends thought me naive to the point of absurdity, nor were they wholly wrong—my appointment to an instructorship in Columbia College was pretty openly regarded as an experiment, and for some time my career in the College was complicated by my being Jewish."[18] At the same time Lewisohn was having his problems at Columbia, Horace Kallen was having similar difficulties at Princeton, and, somewhat later, the poet Stanly Kunitz met with similar rejection at Harvard.[19]

As for Zeitlin's second objection—that Lewisohn exaggerated the provincialism of the Midwest, once one admits, as Zeitlin does, that banality and narrow-mindedness did prevail in Midwestern cities, it is hard to say where exaggeration begins. One does not speak of Sherwood Anderson and Sinclair Lewis as exaggerating.

But, more significantly than its documentation of religious bias and the dangers of mass thinking, *Up Stream* traces a journey into self-knowledge and personal definition, a young man's discovery of self and the setting aside of conventional values. It affirms with passion a liberation from self-deception and deceptions imposed by others. Like Ralph Ellison's novel *Invisible Man*, which also traces a minority figure's progress from accommodation to freedom, it renders this important theme effectively, and so it has a lasting appeal.

Mid-Channel: The Middle Years

Mid-Channel: An American Chronicle (1929), the second of Lewisohn's autobiographies, disappoints when compared to its predecessor. *Up Stream* has a singleness of purpose, the rise and fall of expectations, which places the events of Lewisohn's earlier life in significant order. *Mid-Channel*, though written with equal passion, flings itself about, beginning with a fulminating defense of his personal affairs and concluding with an attack upon Pauline Christianity and an exposition of the leading tenets of Judaism. Sandwiched between are travel sketches, assessments of his own work, often unusually objective, and assessments of other writers, often biased. The chronology of events is lost; the reader has trouble reconstructing the decade under discussion. Parts are often interesting and sometimes valuable, but no sense of the whole comes through.

Before the point at which *Mid-Channel* begins, Lewisohn taught English and Latin briefly at a prep school. Then, in 1919, Oswald Garrison Villard, editor of the *Nation*, offered him the post of drama critic for that periodical. After one year in that service, Lewisohn assumed the desk of associate editor and maintained it until 1924. During this period Lewisohn produced: *A Modern Book of Criticism* (1919), an anthology with an introduction; *The Drama and the Stage* (1922), a valuable selection from his theater reviews published in *The Nation*; and *The Creative Life* (1924), gatherings from articles on general literary principles. Together with *Up Stream*, these works, concerned with broader literary ideas than those written during his teaching career, fist brought him into national attention and made him a figure in the critical swirls of the 1920s.

Also, commencing in 1921 or 1922, Lewisohn entered into a sixteen-year alliance with a young singer, the twenty-year-old Thelma Spear. The legal complexities, the threats of libel suits by Mrs. Mary Crocker Lewisohn (since Lewisohn mined his personal distresses as subject matter for both fiction and autobiography), and the exploitation by newspapers of these events were to torment Lewisohn for many years, well into the 1930s. Of the publicity given his domestic affairs, Lewisohn writes: "...the newspapers, led by those of Mr. Hearst, exploited my severely considered private actions with every device of vulgar flippancy and salacious innuendo...."[20] His difficulties brought Villard, the editor of the *Nation*, as well as Cass Canfield, his editor later at Harper and Brothers, a great deal of pain.

Unable to get a divorce in New York State and afraid of legal prosecution, Lewisohn left his congenial position at the *Nation* and from 1924 spent more than a decade abroad. Miss Spear and he spent nearly a year in Vienna; he made his first trip to Palestine in 1925. In these two years, culminating with the publication of *Israel*, he turned strongly to Judaism and Zionism. In a later interview with Walter Ginsburg in the *Day* (Friday, September 14, 1928), Lewisohn stated that "Mrs. Lewisohn [Thelma Spear], a singer of note, was the first person in Jerusalem to give a vocal concert. She has also contributed much poetry to Anglo-Jewish periodicals." Thelma Spear, he continued, was partly Jewish. In the rest of the interview Lewisohn argued that Jews are different and must accept and benefit from their position as a minority.

After Palestine they then established residence in Paris. Unlike other literary expatriates in Paris at that time, he states, he did not participate actively in Parisian life, but kept himself aloof, witnessing Paris as a spectator. He thought himself more an exile than expatriate. He did not enjoy the company of James Joyce and Ezra Pound, for whose works he had no relish. (Paradoxically, though his judgments on French and German writers were good, his assessment of contemporaries writing in his own tongue was erratic, to say the least.) He states, however, that Paris was quiet, tolerant, and conducive to literary labor.

Contradicting Lewisohn's claim that he led a quiet life in Paris, the English expatriate, boulevardier, and minor man of letters, Sisley Huddleston, in his *Paris Salons, Cafés, Studios* (1928), attests to more exciting days and nights:

Ludwig Lewisohn was my friend and neighbour, and we were constantly in communication. Many evenings did we spend together in the former apartment of George Biddle, the Philadelphia painter. With Thelma Spear as hostess, capital parties which gathered together the French, the German, the Jewish and the American elite of Paris were given. It would fill pages to set down their names. At random I recall Sholom Asch, Marvin Lowenthal, Sinclair Lewis, Theodore Dreiser, Sherwood Anderson, Wells of Harpers, Mala Boshka, the Czechoslovakian singer and pianist, Yvette Guilbert, and her husband Dr. Schiller, Roy Sheldon, the young American sculptor, Myron Nutting, Paul Burlin, Jan Hambourg, the violinist, Regis Michaud, the French professor who gave up his post in America to spread the fame of American writers in France, Thomas Mann, Ernst Toller, Lee Simsonson, Cyril and Evelyn Scott, Georg Frederic Hummel, Manuel Komroff, and other German and American novelists, the Franco-Jewish composer, Leon Algazi, the musician Albert Jarosy, Horace Kallen, the Jewish-American philosopher, Ivan and Clair Goll, who write in several languages, Paul Robeson, the negro singer, Ladislav Medgyes, stage-designer, Padraic and Mary Colum, Joseph Bard, Freda Kirchwey of the Nation, Irita Van Doren of Books, Léon Bazalgette, translator of Whitman, Oko, the great Hebraist, Elmer Rice, the playwright ... I forget half of them but I mention these because they convey an idea of the varied and vivid company of the Montparnasse days. It was always good to be with the Lewisohns but it was best when Thelma sang. She has a rich golden voice, intelligently trained; and she held us spell-bound when she consented to sing Negro or German or Jewish folk songs. Surely it is a pity that she has been compelled to choose between a concert career and a domestic existence; yet I cannot but approve her choice of domestic existence. What the platform has lost, hearts and a hearth have gained.[21]

The time covered by *Mid-Channel* (from about 1924 to 1929, the first part of his residence abroad) proved the apex of his literary career. In this period Lewisohn wrote, in addition to other work, four of his best books: *The Case of Mr. Crump* (1926), a minor masterpiece, a piercing autobiographical novel brilliantly dissecting an unhappy marriage, written with an icy self-control; *Cities and Men* (1927), an impressive critical work, with brief but insightful, sometimes magisterial, glimpses into the lives and writings of such varied figures as Hazlitt, Mann, Rilke, Buber, Heine, and Baudelaire; *The Island Within* (1928), a poignant novel imbued with irony, a turning point in American Jewish fiction, dramatizing the dangers of assimilation and inter-marriage; and *Israel* (1925), an informed book of travel to Germany, Austria, Poland, and Palestine, almost prophetic of future events. In these four works Lewisohn rises to an elevation of vision and style he had not attained before and was only occasionally to achieve again.

The Case of Mr. Crump had a tortuous publishing history. No American publisher would accept it, for it seemed to invite costly libel suits. In 1926 Edward Titus, an American bibliophile living in Paris and an admirer of the manuscript, published at his own cost an expensive limited edition with an excellent introduction by Thomas Mann. The edition was quickly snatched up by readers, and the book praised by Freud, Theodore Dreiser, and Sinclair Lewis.

The American Post Office, presumably because of a few provocative pages, forebade its entry into the United States. Only in 1947 was an American firm, Farrar, Straus, and Cudahy, willing to publish it. The *New Yorker*, in 1947, commented: "This masterly novel about a hideous marriage is now published in this country for the first time. After a generation, this story is just as horrifying—and as entertaining—as it was when the smuggled French edition fluttered the literary dovecotes of the twenties."[22] Later, an abridged version, under the title *The Tyranny of Sex*, was put out in paperback by the New American Library and proved to be a popular seller.

Mrs. Lewisohn's litigiousness is attested to in an anecdote in Joseph Wood Krutch's memoir *More Lives Than One.* He had casually mentioned on the radio that he had originally become the *Nation's* drama critic because Lewisohn, his predecessor, could not get along with his wife. On returning home, Krutch was called to the phone; the caller, the first Mrs. Lewisohn, exclaimed angrily that she had been libeled and threatened legal action.[23]

The difficulties of publishing and circulating the book in the twenties added to Lewisohn's feelings of persecution at that time. In hindsight, it might appear that Lewisohn invited martyrdom, but he states that he always wrote or acted with motives of the highest moral idealism; certainly his writings display an idealistic sensibility. Stanley F. Chyet comments sympathetically:

Defeat and torment haunted him—a bitter misalliance with his first wife, a Gentile twenty years his senior; the grief of seeing *The Broken Snare,* his first novel, expressed as subversive of Victorian morality; the need to endure obloquy in World War I America for his exposition of modern German literature (his probings of French poetry were shunted aside) and his advocacy at the Ohio State University of a pacifist standpoint; the wasting away of his parents and their hopes of his success; the withdrawal into madness of his soulmate William Ellery Leonard; obstacles of a formidable sort to a respectable union with a young woman for whom he had left his wife; a decade-long expatriation to Europe, and, in America, the banning of his *magnum opus, The Case of Mr. Crump.*[24]

In Vienna Lewisohn had discovered Sigmund Freud, who subsequently exerted a strong influence upon him, notably in *The Island Within* and *Expression in America.* More significant for him, during his "exile," was his return to Judaism, the result, in part, of his disappointment with Germany and the anti-Semitism he found there. He also made a new commitment to Zionism, German-Jewish in origin, abetted by his meetings with Dr. Chaim Weizmann and Kurt Blumenfeld, the "leader of the German Zionists," and by his reading of Martin Buber. He concludes *Mid-Channel* with an attack on Pauline Christianity, which he identifies with American Puritanism in its rejection of the senses, and proclaims his admiration for Judaism, which makes allowances for both the spiritual and the physical.

Whatever the virtues or shortcomings of his theology, one notes the parallels between his thought and his life. Raised in an American Protestant setting that he believed to have failed him, he turned more and more to an ethnic identification which provided him with greater security and authenticated his position as an outsider. More narrowly, the laws governing divorce in New York and other states, an emblem of Christian resistance to divorce, contrasted with the more liberal attitudes of Judaism in this regard.

Contemporary reviews of *Mid-Channel* understandably found it a letdown after *Up Stream*. Less exciting—such was the verdict of Robert Morss Lovett, in *Bookman* (June 1929). Irwin Edman, in the *Nation* (June 5, 1929), admired its succinct accounts of literary figures, but wrote that "the early part of this book was a little too full of Mr. Lewisohn's past marital difficulties and his present domestic felicity."[25] Edman was not impressed with Lewisohn's proposals for finding salvation in Judaism. A savage review was Henry Hazlitt's in the *New York Evening Sun* (April 27, 1929), which called Lewisohn a moral prig, full of self-pity. Hazlitt believed that, for one advocating tolerance, Lewisohn was insufficiently tolerant of Christianity. The Jewish ethical tradition, Hazlitt wrote, for Lewisohn is "essentially joyous, anti-Puritanical, anti-ascetic, teaching always peace, tolerance, sweetness, gentleness, love"; but Hazlitt thought Judaism as fallible as Christianity. Hazlitt conceded the book's fine literary touches and its rich prose. Reviewers in smaller cities and in Jewish journals were more sympathetic.

In retrospect, the weakness of *Mid-Channel* is not its materials—the period covered was at least as eventful as his earlier years—but its lack of structure. The book has no center, no climax. How and why Lewisohn returned to Judaism and became a foe of assimilation, for example, is not clearly discussed. Lewisohn might have chosen as a model John Henry Newman's elegant and well-organized *Apologia*.

Haven: Decline in Reputation

Haven (1940), written jointly by Lewisohn and Edna, his second wife, is the last of the three autobiographies; like the second, it is a work of mixed merit. It interests as a saddening account of a decline of literary power, though missing the objectivity of F. Scott Fitzgerald's *Crack-Up* (1945, posthumously edited by Edmund Wilson). This decline is partially covered by the domestic happiness Lewisohn states he has now found with Edna Manley, whom he married in February, 1940.

Haven, which covers less than a year in Lewisohn's life, is written in letter and diary form, with alternating sections by Lewisohn and his new wife. The entries written by Edna Lewisohn are feminine, intelligent, and worshipful of her husband; her idolatry might have been a needed prop for his vanity, damaged by the growing neglect of both critics and public. Her entries add an everyday account of bourgeois domesticity which lends a welcome Pepysian detail.

Born in Rochester, New York, in 1908, Edna Manley had been educated at William Smith College and Beaver College. She had gained writing experience as a newspaperwoman. Briefly married and divorced, she had suffered, in 1936, a breakdown. She had met Lewisohn in October, 1938, after his New York divorce from Mary Crocker Lewisohn, and, following her conversion to Judaism, had married him in Baltimore.

The occasion of their marriage coincided with an acrimonious struggle in the courts between Lewisohn and Thelma Spear over the custody of their son, James Elias, born September 17, 1933, Lewisohn's only child. (The mother was awarded custody of the child in 1941). Edna Manley Lewisohn writes that Lewisohn contested custody on the grounds that Thelma had refused to marry him: "Hence, when in the summer and fall of 1937, L.L. being at last free to do so, was able to offer her marriage and did so on repeated occasions before a variety of witnesses, she refused that offer, again in the interests of her career, with unmistakable emphasis. The matter of the legitimation of the child was evidently of no concern to her then."[26] Lewisohn's comments on

Thelma Spear are as bitter as his earlier references to her had been glowing. Krutch wrote in his memoir that Lewisohn "celebrated the beauty of monogamy through a series of marriages each of which was defended as the only *true* marriage it had been his good fortune to achieve."[27]

In the Byronic mode, Lewisohn bore the pageant of his bleeding heart publicly. He frequently cited, in different works, an author's life as the source of literature; but one wonders, while reading *Haven*, whether Lewisohn had not transgressed the limits of publishable autobiography. In his later years he was to declare that *Haven* was not part of his "canon" (as cited by Harold U. Ribalow in conversation with this author). But he had published the work years before.

In 1940 Lewisohn was concerned about his increasing loss of popularity as a writer, as registered both in reviews and in sales volume. This decline commenced with the novel *Stephen Escott* (1930), and continued through *The Last Days of Shylock* (1931), *Trumpet of Jubilee* (1937), and *Forever Wilt Thou Love* (1939). *Expression in America* (1932), a literary history of the United States, met with generally favorable reviews, but its comparative success did not compensate for the lack of attention shown his novels. Once, in 1940, after attending a tea with Edmund Wilson and Mrs. Marshall, literary editor of the *Nation*, he lamented to a friend, "They don't read me, Saul." Another time, more angrily, he states that "my exclusion from that Oxford Book [of American writers] is a son-of-a-bitch's trick, attributable to the most brutal malice" (250).

Lewisohn set up several defenses to bolster his ego. First, he proclaimed the superiority of his more recent work to his better-received books of the 1920s. His more recent novels, he writes, did not mark a decline in creative power, but rather an advance, characterized by greater density and intellectual complexity, not yet appreciated by the public. The public wanted "Zola; I aim after Racine." Second, he seems to resent the continued popularity of his earlier works, almost as though he were jealous of them. An example: *"The Island Within* is due to appear in the Modern Library on April 3. It is far from being my favorite among my novels and hence retrospectively (with rueful humor) I grudge its extreme and lasting popularity..." (100). Third, his appraisals of contemporaries who had apparently not fallen by the wayside, like Joyce and Sinclair Lewis, are belittling. (All the more painful to contemplate when one recalls that Lewisohn had early championed Sinclair Lewis[28] and had written, when in Paris, Sylvia Beach recalls, the letter of protest objecting to the publishing piracy of Joyce's *Ulysses* before its formal publication; the letter had been signed by hundreds.)[29]

In *Haven* his disappointments were partially disguised by his notion of new married bliss, but he occasionally expresses regret for the mistakes of his past. Once, though he usually mentioned his father tenderly, he laments his father's philosophical materialism, which had given him a false direction, and his father's lack of opposition to his first marriage on grounds of disparities both in age and religion.

Last Years

Some of Lewisohn's best work in his last decade is polemical, such as *The American Jew* (1950), arguing against religious assimilation and for the preserving of ethnic identity; these works necessarily had interest only for smaller audiences. Yet it is a simplification to say, as some have done,[30] that the growing intensity of his commitment to Zionism and Judaism in his last fifteen years led to his decline of creative power. Earlier works with Jewish content (*Israel, The Island Within*) are among his best; later works, such as *Anniversary* (1948), without Jewish content, are weak. The ebb of creativity, like its full tide, is often difficult to understand and must often be accepted simply as a "given."

Partially to supplement his income as an author with failing sales, Lewisohn resorted to the lecture trail, addressing Jewish groups. Sam Friedman, who arranged his lectures for the Jewish Welfare Board in New York, remembers him as an excellent lecturer—always articulate and fluent, always reliable, though humorless. Inaugurating about 1940, a weekly column, "The

Watchman," in the *New Palestine*, a journal sponsored by the Zionist Organization of America, Lewisohn assumed the editorship of that publication in 1943 and maintained it until 1948. He had married again, to the former Miss Louise Wolk, in February, 1944. In 1948 he was appointed professor of Comparative Literature at Brandeis University, his first teaching post in thirty years, and in 1955 was named University Librarian. While vacationing in Miami Beach, he suffered a heart attack, and four days later, on December 31, 1955, at the Miami Beach Heart Institute, he died. He had been writing busily till almost the end.

An impression of these last years is rendered by his son, James Elias Lewisohn, in *Midstream* magazine.[31] The son was a student at Brandeis when his father taught there. The picture drawn has the ambivalence, the stern yet loving regard, one would expect of many sons writing about their fathers. The son had found Lewisohn a gentle and understanding father, but difficult to get along with because of the older man's all-consuming theology. James did not share the view he correctly attributes to his father: "The Jew as the chosen tool of complete redemption for an unredeemed world consumed the man, who, with a truly Renaissance mind, had mastered many literatures and cultures."

Lewisohn gave his son much trouble about dating Gentile girls though he himself had married two. The son records that Lewisohn had a wretched time living with his personal contradictions. He was constantly preoccupied with thoughts of repentance for "our many separations, his matrimonial flops, and, lastly, his impieties." As for kosher rituals: "There would he sit, apologizing to me for using milk in his coffee after a meat meal and trying imperfectly to speed through the *amidah* at the pace of the Orthodox Jews he so admired and envied." Lewisohn thus evinced the difficulties of turning to religious orthodoxy in one's later years.

Among undergraduates he proved an engaging teacher, mixing literary judgments with anecdotes of Paris and of nights spent with James Joyce (seen now, apparently, in a mellower light). He had a fantastic memory, his son recalls, and could recite, if challenged over martinis, the second part of *Faust*, three books of *Paradise Lost*, the entire Catholic High Mass in Latin.

As a summing up, in his article James Lewisohn writes: "If his judgments were often those of passionate intensity as opposed to more incumbent reasons, if his limitations were many, he still sought truth, not triumph. I never knew him to be calculatingly cruel or fervently unjust either as a man, a father, a teacher, or friend...."

Chapter Two
Novels of Love and Marriage

In a literary career spanning almost half a century, Ludwig Lewisohn wrote fifteen novels and a collection of novellas, *This People* (1933). He was, in the 1940s, to regard himself primarily as a novelist, despite the abundant criticism he had written. His novels are realistic, in the manner of conventional late-nineteenth or early-twentieth century fiction, and sometimes "naturalistic," a term he used to indicate a nondoctrinaire but bold confrontation with unpleasant truth. (In 1914 Lewisohn wrote: "Today naturalism means probity of observation merely. In 1890 it meant the literary expression of scientific positivism.")[1] His novels often are *thesis* novels, a legitimate genre, though not much practiced today. *The Island Within* (1928) is his most successful thesis novel; *The Case of Mr. Crump* (1926) is his best "naturalistic" novel, imbued, to a degree unusual for Lewisohn, with a passionate grasp of character—in Hazlitt's term, with a "gusto" for characterization.

Ten of these novels are primarily non-Jewish in content and are concerned with love and marital discord. His third novel among these, *The Case of Mr. Crump*, is the most autobiographical, detailed, and gripping. If *The Broken Snare* and *Don Juan* may be thought of as apprentice work, the three following *Mr. Crump* show a slackening of technique and a vitiating tendency to moralize at length but still retain some power. The novels commencing with *An Altar in the Fields* (1931)—the last four—range from the mediocre to the trivial. After 1931 Lewisohn had pretty much exhausted his subject matter and had lost involvement with character, story, setting.

Before *Mr. Crump*

Lewisohn's first novel, *The Broken Snare* (1908), dedicated to his first wife, was written as an effort to escape menial writing

26

tasks. Although a very early work, it seems no worse than several of his later novels—perhaps because, except for *Mr. Crump*, which ranges far above his usual level, Lewisohn made no serious attempt later to advance himself in the techniques of fiction. He always seemed content with his earliest models, such as the stories of William Dean Howells and the early Henry James; as novelist he did not work hard enough at his art.

Reasonably well constructed, with a good prose style, *The Broken Snare* nevertheless fails to move the reader. Insufficiently infused with imaginative intensity, its temperature, like much of Lewisohn's fiction, is tepid. The work is pervaded with a melancholy Lewisohn must have felt at the time of its writing, a sadness that does not always have an "objective correlative." Frances, the heroine, never is happy, even at the peak of her love for Julian. The novel glooms with the somber twilights of Morningside Heights brownstones and the still dignity and decadence of Queenshaven (Charleston).

Frances Gannett, age twenty-four, feels her "repressed vitality," the constraints placed upon her by her parents and her environment. Her parents' marriage is unhappy—the first of Lewisohn's pictures of marital strife—and Mrs. Gannett's struggle with genteel poverty in Manhattan "had made of her body a rag, and of her soul a bundle of vulgar anxieties."[2] She has no sympathy for her husband, a scientist of strict principles, and only laments his shortcomings as a breadwinner. In Mrs. Gannett we find the first of the author's misogynous portraits of querulous and domineering wives. Frances takes consolation in books and art and seeks vaguely for a religious faith, a "Church and its visible symbols." If we draw inference from Frances, Lewisohn never entirely abandoned his childhood leaning toward religion.

Frances falls in love with Julian Ware, a writer and intellectual, who reciprocates her feeling but will not marry her because of his lack of faith in the institution, a result of his own parents' unhappy marriage. (As one newly married, the author seems unusually concerned with the theme of marital discord.) Ware's theories prevail over Frances's doubts, and they elope to Queenshaven, unmarried. So far, this was fairly strong stuff for American readers in 1908, not long after Theodore Dreiser's publishing difficulties with *Sister Carrie* (1900).

After Frances becomes pregnant, her mother dies and the girl is left with enormous guilt; she turns severely ill and aborts. Lewisohn's essentially middle-class point of view asserts itself. Frances reflects upon her unmarried state: "... it came to her, with new and terrible force, that their sin was being visited upon them; that all suffering sprang from the bond approved and tested by the ages and required by the laws of God and men."[3] After Frances loses the child, Julian suddenly surrenders his convictions to his feelings and wants to marry her.

Neither Julian's initial arguments against marriage nor his conversion at the end seem convincing. Paradoxically, the book is filled with marital discord, yet sees marriage as a necessary convention; "free love" leads inevitably to suffering and religious guilt. Lewisohn masks his own confusion with much purple writing at the end of the novel. If *The Broken Snare* is an example of "naturalistic" writing, as the author describes it, it lacks the greater integrity of the really "naturalistic" *Sister Carrie*.

Incidentally, in this first novel, Lewisohn already manifests his dislike of literary coteries and parties. His fictional spokesmen usually regard such groups as effete, hermaphroditic, and insincere. Lewisohn usually had real-life counterparts in mind, and, like D. H. Lawrence, he preferred people outside a consciously literary setting.

Don Juan (1923), written in twenty-nine days and published fifteen years later, during which time Lewisohn had devoted himself to literary criticism and scholarship, stems from an autobiographical impulse. As a thesis novel, it attacked the difficulty of securing a divorce in New York State, where divorce was possible only if the marriage partners were willing to enter into a collusion to establish adultery as grounds. (This New York law prevailed until well after World War II.) The novel, aside from its thesis, describes the agonizing of an unhappily married man, in love with a young woman not his wife, and caught in a trap of law and convention from which he cannot escape.

In *Mid-Channel* Lewisohn commented of *Don Juan*: "The story dealt, of course, with the conflict in which I was involved.

The conflict absorbed me wholly; I could think of nothing else. I stripped it, however, of the very special elements of my own case and placed it among rather uncomplicated higher middle-class Americans...."[4] Though superior to his first novel in intensity and interest, *Don Juan* is neither as close to the circumstances of Lewisohn's own case as *The Case of Mr. Crump* nor as successful a novel.

The domineering character of Anne Crump, Lewisohn's greatest literary creation, is reduced in this earlier novel to a less imposing wifely figure, Elise. Elise is less monstrous as a character, but also less absorbing. In *Don Juan*, too, the autobiographical elements of age difference and of step-children are omitted; the issue is defined simply as incompatibility.

Elise, married nine years to Lucien Curtis, will not grant him a divorce and uses every resource and stratagem available to her to preserve their marriage. She takes the unreasonable position that her marriage is worth keeping even if her husband does not love or want her. Lucien, in love with Helga, sees in Helga's eyes "neither question nor compulsion nor reproach nor discontent nor a provocative pathos nor any appeal nor any desire to draw anything from him or change anything within him."[5] Lewisohn often seems to expect a wife to be completely without demands, more an idol-worshiper than a human being.

Elise, on the other hand, to Lucien "had in the life of love the horse-hair primness, arrogance, fear of giving of the long-skirted lady of mid-Victorian fiction at its tawdriest" (*DJ*, 20). Here, too, Elise differs from Anne Crump, whose Victorian ladylike exterior masks a sexual aggressiveness bordering on nymphomania. Elise's greatest weapon in confronting the world is that she is "not guilty." As innocent victim, she presents a picture of woe, of the maltreated wife, to an all-too-sympathetic audience, including Lucien's father.

In his puritanical social setting Lucien is the offender, the "Don Juan." He cannot elope with Helga, with whom he has maintained only a platonic love, because elopement would give her a bad name, especially in "her little New England town," and would devastate Helga's mother. Lucien's dilemma has no solution. He contemplates putting a gun to his head; this thought of suicide anticipates the murder which ends a similar dilemma in *The Case of Mr. Crump*. Lucien finally rejects the idea of suicide.

Society advocates, Lucien learns, standard compromises even at the expense of love and feeling. Arrayed against him are his wife, his father, Helga's mother, Elise's sister—a battle-axe of conventionality—and even his own fear of gossip overwhelming Helga. He finds some intellectual solace in conversations with the painter Blaffka, modeled after Dreiser, and the cynical Dornheim, who presents H. L. Mencken's point of view. He finds temporary sexual solace with Grace, a modern, worldly woman, who can enjoy sex without love or marriage—an attitude the middle-class man and romantic in Lucien or Lewisohn cannot share for long. At the end, Lucien decides to leave his wife and go to Europe, his relationship with Helga unresolved.

The characteristic tensions in Lewisohn's novels first reveal themselves in *Don Juan*. An idealist who will not accept marriage without love, he also spurns love, or at least sex, without marriage. Advocating a liberalization of the divorce laws, he also dislikes the modern "liberated" woman and seeks in woman an Oriental posture. Lucien reflects: "He was willing to adore, to worship his woman for her charm, her loving-kindness, her serviceableness, her song, her dance. He was not willing to treat her as an equal in judgment, power, decision . . . he was not" (*DJ*, 133-34).

A better work than its predecessor, *Don Juan* remains more a tract than a novel, more given to argument than anything else. Henry Seidel Canby, in the *Nation*, reviewed it as a "brilliant" piece of special pleading, not a novel: "Mr. Lewisohn has imagined a situation in which the husband is absolutely right in wishing to be divorced, provided that one grants that it is right for him to follow the only course in which he can be human, happy, and useful to himself or anyone."[6]

The Case of Mr. Crump: His Masterpiece

Instead of leaving his wife and going off to Europe alone, as did Lucien Curtis in *Don Juan*, Lewisohn went off to Europe with

Thelma Spear, leaving, as he had feared, eddies of notoriety in his wake. His next novel, his third, written in Europe in four and one-half months and published in a limited edition of 500 copies in 1926, was *The Case of Mr. Crump*—a work which, covering some of the same autobiographical ground as *Don Juan*, runs far ahead of it in value. It is difficult to explain this sudden eruption of the exceptional after mediocrity. Could writing on European ground have proven liberating? From a distance, perhaps, the author could face the truths of his own life more openly. Whatever the reason, *Mr. Crump* is Lewisohn's best "naturalistic" novel, one of the distinctive novels written by an American in the 1920s, the one posterity should preserve after shedding the others discussed in this chapter.

Thomas Mann, in his original 1926 Preface, stressed that the work is documentary or autobiographical: "...simultaneously and at every moment the book is more and less than a novel; it is life, it is concrete and undreamed reality and its artistic silence seems in more than one passage desperately like a cry. Yet the content somehow does not shatter the aesthetic form or the work's artistic values."[7]

The Preface, one of the most important critical statements on Lewisohn and deserving extended quotation, continues: "We have here, then, a novelistic document of life, of the *inferno* of a marriage....It is American conditions that are delineated.... One must grant that his power to stir and entertain us is very great. His book stands in the very forefront of modern epic narrative. His style is manly, sincere, precise and strong; there is in it a high determination after compact and direct truth..." (*CC*, vii-viii). Mann correctly traces likenesses to August Strindberg's work and to Strindberg's "dry and desperate humor." The characters are all believable human beings; even Anne Crump, repulsive as she is, remains human and understandable in her compulsions.

Finally, Mann stresses *The Case of Mr. Crump* as an attempt to liberalize attitudes toward love and marriage in America, though he thinks Europeans should also heed the book's message without complacency. Mann classifies Lewisohn with Sinclair Lewis,

Mencken, Judge Lindsey, and others "who are striving to transform the handsome, energetic children of American civilization into beings of a ripe and adult culture" (*CC*, viii). But the world has become smaller, and the problems the novel faces transgress national boundaries. "Lewisohn declares at the close of his story that he desired to appeal 'to the heart of mankind himself.' He shall not have made, nor would I willingly suffer him to have made, this appeal in vain" (*CC*, viii).

Lewisohn's thesis is stated clearly in his own postscript to his work: "... in the present state of public opinion in America and of a man's professional and economic dependence on that opinion, the wife holds dice so heavily loaded from the beginning that any vulgar and unscrupulous woman may unresistedly ruin any man whom, by any means, she can lure or force into a marriage ceremony."[8]

But *Mr. Crump* impresses not because of its thesis but because it is a ripe work of fiction: dense in detail, expertly organized, effective in dialogue, for a change, and in characterization. Despite the autobiographical content, the novel has artistic detachment, permitting the story itself, rather than editorializing, to persuade the reader. Sharing Mr. Crump's idealism, the novelist has the reader see this idealism tarnished amid the daily crises of a bad, foolish marriage; the clash of wills is shown in the cruel light of truth.

Book I, titled "Anne," traces Anne Bronson Vilas Crump's history prior to meeting and marrying Herbert Crump, twenty years her junior, as Crump later pieces her story together in listening to her reminiscences over the years of their marriage. Her family background is sordid, with the men on both sides of her family generally shiftless and ineffectual, and the women, in order to survive without much male support, scheming and sexually opportunistic. Anne Crump's heredity is "coarse and violent," the women engaged constantly in battle of the sexes and the seeking of revenge against men. The one redeeming quality of the Bronson women is their almost primitive and belligerent protection of offspring and even of parents. Married to a feckless gambler, Harrison Vilas, and with three children, Anne does not hesitate to seduce the young composer, Herbert Crump, who seems a better prospect for a steady marriage.

Once Crump and she are married (Book III and later), the family pattern of behavior asserts itself in her. She constantly gives priority to her children's demands, no matter how irrational, ignoring her husband's musical aspirations and his financial limits. Her sexual passion, which at first tyrannizes over him, later turns to a possessive jealousy against the possibility of his straying; she even hires private detectives to watch him. Her life is stained by turmoil, slovenliness, shamelessness, and guile. Her upbringing has taught her not to love her husband, but to view him as a necessary and unavoidable opponent. Her essential coarseness is usually disguised by a certain outer refinement, which accompanies a genuine, though not penetrating, love of literature. Privately, she often breaks out into obscenity and abuse.

Book II follows Herbert Crump (originally *Krumpf*) through his childhood and early manhood. Born into a musical family which has migrated from Germany to Queenshaven (Charleston), Crump has inherited his family's musical talent but has dropped its traditional Lutheran piety, already weakened in his parents. His grandfather, in Herbert's childhood, comments that he has talent but no respect for God. Herbert is descended from a long line of church organists. Lewisohn laments apparently a break in a long chain of religious adherence and the loss of an art consecrated to religion.

Lewisohn, of course, identifies with Crump both emotionally and sympathetically. The author's knowledge of classical music is broad enough to display his protaganist successfully as a serious composer. All the Jewish components of Lewisohn's life, in this autobiographical fiction, are eliminated except for Anne Crump's anti-Semitic outbursts—not directly aimed at Crump—late in the novel.

Herbert's father is a man of troubled and frustrated spirit; abandoning the faith of his ancestors, he "hungered for the ineffable and the infinite.... Science had cooled his head while romanticism had heated his heart." Herbert's mother, who tended toward a brooding melancholy, yearned for her native Vienna. Both feel unadjusted in the New World.

The young Crump shares the sexual yearnings of his schoolfellows; but whereas most Southern boys of his acquaintance had their sexual initiation with young mulatto or black girls, Herbert's shyness and diffidence, together with the friendly feeling his family shared for blacks, unlike the rest of the white community, prevented Herbert's erotic urges from finding such an outlet. His long-tried virginity helps make him an easy prey, in his twenties, to Anne Vilas.

In New York, at the beginning of his career, Crump falls in love with Gerda, a beautiful girl with Viennese musical training, whose ambition is to succeed in operettas and marry a millionaire. She dismisses Crump as a suitor, with insight, as both an "idealist and philistine," out of step with her own goals. Shortly after, he meets Mrs. Vilas on the rebound, and though much of her appearance and behavior repel him, he succumbs to her sexual accessibility and lack of restraint. He has at least one inkling of her duplicity, but chooses to ignore it. Anne's mother, Mrs. Toohey, lives with her, and Crump discovers that Anne has revealed their relationship to her mother.

A remnant of prudence in him registered a psychical protest when, from the veiled allusions of the two women, he discoverd that Mrs. Toohey was privy to the relations between Anne and himself. The old woman ate Vilas' bread and yet Anne had dared to tell her! From this alone a whiff of moral corruption should have reached him. Steeped in his false romance, persuaded by his nobler pity for Anne to find or make excuses, lulled by the harem ceremonial of the hour, he hushed the monitions of his soul.... "(CC, 86).

Crump would have been better off, the author reflects, if he had resorted to New York prostitutes, accessible at Columbus Circle at that time.

She demands marriage and proves relentless in pursuit, to the extent of following him to his parents' home in Queenshaven. His old-fashioned parents, taken in by her air of refinement and deeming pre-marital relationships to be a marriage contract, do not discourage her. She receives a divorce in Illinois through legal chicanery and fraud and, ultimately, largely because of Crump's youthful weakness and inexperience, succeeds in marrying him.

To accomplish her end, she alternates tactics of terrorizing him and throwing herself on his mercy. At one point she appeals to his pity:

> She caught his arm. "Then you do love me and I won't have to die?"
> He softened to her. She did love him; she must love him—hopelessly and overwhelmingly. "No, dear Anne, of course I don't want you to die."
> "I thought you did, Herbert. Oh, I thought you really did." (CC, 116).

A composer in his twenties, trying to fulfill his gifts, he finds himself in a domestic hell, in which desires have no restraints, inhabited by an unruly wife and mother; a son almost his own age given to drink and gambling; a manic-depressive, sometimes hospitalized, older daughter; and a younger daughter, the only one in the family Crump likes but who, in a turbulent upbringing, has become sad and sullen. Crump composes, despite unsettling conditions, works of permanent value. To help earn a living, he takes a position at a college of music in Central City, Ohio.

He dreams of having a wife his own age and of having his own children. In one scene, sitting at the deathbed of his father, Crump reflects: "... he was considering with an immeasurable pain within, a pain that reached after and questioned fate itself, how different, how really sweet and mellow life could have been for his father and mother if he had married an ordinarily suitable, kind, helpful mother of children of his own" (CC, 228). His longing for a normal married life mingles here with guilt over the damage the turns of his life had inflicted upon his parents.

At the end, he falls in love with a young singer, Barbara Trent, and he expresses his wish to leave his wife for her. But the implacable Mrs. Crump threatens him with scandal, with newspaper stories of "love nests," and with financial ruin, all of which had been the lot of a literary friend of his (in real life, Harry Thurston Peck). At the climax of a violent quarrel, in sudden

rage, he kills her with a poker. He is sent to prison for
manslaughter.

The ending of the novel reflects the fact that Lewisohn's own
relationship with his wife, at the time the novel was written, was
not yet emotionally or legally resolved. In the book Crump feels
no guilt for his wife's death. What he has done, though horrible,
is better than the tortuous dilemma that could find no other
solution:

> Quietly he went to the window and opened it and looked up at the
> stars. If the universe was a mere mechanism and we but accidental
> crawlers on the planet's crest, neither deeds done or undone mattered-
> ....But if this were not so, if...the universe strove, like man himself,
> for values beyond the dust, then he had helped to reestablish the shaken
> moral equilibrium of the world, to save cosmos from chaos, to make
> justice to prevail. Though his body would be imprisoned, his mind
> would be free....He turned and looked at that huddled, shrunken,
> sack-like bundle on the floor. Where now were her gibes and her
> malevolence and her ferocity, her lusts and treacheries and hates?...
> How strong and unvanquishable she had been....Goodness might have
> made her almost great. Evil is both destroyer and destroyed....Slowly
> he went to the telephone, took up the receiver and asked for police
> headquarters. (CC, 310-11).

Crump had contemplated suicide intermittently, like Lucien in
Don Juan, but finally committed a homicide. Suicide and murder,
of course, are inverted images of each other. During his years of
marital turmoil Crump's music had helped him to bear his life.
But his marriage was too hellish, his yearning for normal life too
strong, for music alone to sustain him permanently.

The book, of course, was not printed in the United States
because of the fear on the part of publishers of libel suits. As late
as 1946, the year of the first Mrs. Lewisohn's death, publishers
were afraid to issue it for fear of libel suits at the behest of her
children. In 1926, in addition to its invitation to law suits, the
book displayed an unusual frankness about the intimate details of
marriage, though never in the least obscene.

Mr. Crump is perhaps unrivaled as a close view of the torments
of a bad marriage and deserves greater recognition than it pres-

ently enjoys. Sigmund Freud called it "an incomparable master-piece";[9] Sinclair Lewis stated it "has the strength, lucidity and nobility of great literature."[10] Joseph Wood Krutch, reviewing it in the *Nation*, described *The Case of Mr. Crump* as a "hideously powerful novel."[11] Mencken, in the *American Mercury*, argued for the essential morality of the book: "It is soberly composed, devoid of the usual novelist's tricks, and full of excellent writing." Mencken also praised the depiction of Mrs. Crump: "Even Lewisohn's Jezebel is an assiduous and almost immolating mother. She wrecks her husband that her atrocious children may survive."[12] The *Times Literary Supplement* (London, August 20, 1931) called it "an extremely powerful book" and an "indictment of American public opinion." Of Anne Crump, the reviewer wrote: "Anne Crump, though not inhuman, is a being of complete moral chaos; she is impervious to any appeal, she is a physical and moral slattern of indomitable will, and nothing but physical destruction can destroy her power over her husband." Mrs. Crump evidences the fact that a literary character can be born out of intense hatred as well as out of love.

Somewhat more neutral in his appraisal of the work is Frederick J. Hoffman, who, in *Freudianism and the Literary Mind*, wrote: "*The Case of Mr. Crump*, one of the ugliest books of modern literature, tells the story of a brilliant and sensitive artist, a composer, who has been forced to live in unholy wedlock with a woman twice his age, who will not divorce him and who drives him ultimately to a horrible murder."[13] The impartial reader, I think, will agree that the power, the restraint, and the insight of the novel overbalance the "ugliness" of its subject matter.

Roman Summer and *Stephen Escott*: American Dilemmas

Novels of love and marriage following *Mr. Crump* are *Roman Summer* (1927) and *Stephen Escott* (1930). Both attempt to deal objectively with the problems of marriage in America, to take them out of the realm of the author's own tribulations. Both are comparatively anemic, lacking the *felt* experience of their predecessor. Lewisohn often argued that the source of all good literature was autobiographical; the weaknesses of these two novels indicate that the generalization often held true for him, at least.

Roman Summer also deals with the dilemmas of the American writer. John Austin, age thirty-two, a native of Columbus, Ohio, feels spiritually exhausted, in need of renewal. He is a mild and provincial man of letters. His vision of life in the Midwest and his writing practices do not square. His vision is realistic; his writing tradition, genteel: "His living city filled his vision; from his pen dripped a diluted perfume of withered roses."[14] Like the early Lewisohn, "At college he had fallen under the influence of a teacher of intense but limited and stagnant tastes...a favorite pupil of George Edward Woodberry, a protegé of Richard Watson Gilder in the genteel days of *The Century* ..." (*RS*, 7). Austin, himself, though young, wrote "like a secluded and elderly gentleman in an English garden." He had been strongly influenced by his mother, a woman of superior intellect but without emotional depth. At one point Austin exclaims to his mother: "Unless you're a rowdy, American life doesn't give you a chance at the sort of experience that the artist needs. And the fellows who have lived rowdy lives and have the material, haven't the form and just stammer" (*RS*, 35–36). Later, Austin is to side with Dreiser and the "rowdies," the Redskins as against the Palefaces. Austin's literary development parallels Lewisohn's.

In an interesting interlude, while his mother spends a winter away, Austin rents a room with the Earnharts, a family Lewisohn chose to represent an aspect of the American tragedy: The ambitious mother, with an only, unmarried daughter, lives far beyond her husband's means. When her husband discovers that his income will be garnished because of debts he is unaware of, he goes berserk. The Earnharts constitute the subject about which Austin, at the end of *Roman Summer*, will write his first novel. The Earnhart episode—a disguised version of certain events in *The Case of Mr. Crump*—is in Lewisohn's best "naturalistic" vein, and Lewisohn correctly assessed, in *Mid-Channel*, that the Earnharts are the most striking feature of *Roman Summer*. He also admitted that Austin himself lacks vitality as a character. The young Lionel Trilling, in his *Menorah Journal* review (1928), found both Austin and Esther Azancot—the second important character in the book—unconvincing: "Insistently we feel we are reading about John Austin; there is never any present tense, never any flame of immediacy. We know always that he is a symbol. It is Esther Azancot, however, who is most disappointing. We expect a better Jewess from Mr. Lewisohn."[15]

Austin goes to Europe on a quest for self-discovery. There he meets the Brawleys, a restive American professor, bound in the shackles of academic timidity, and his unimaginative wife, both of whom are well sketched. They portray the hacks of academe, as Lewisohn saw them in Midwestern universities.

More important, Austin meets a mysterious and attractive young woman, later revealed as the Jewish Esther Azancot. With Esther, Lewisohn introduces for the first time in his fiction a Jewish theme—evidence that his sense of Jewishness was first fiercely aroused during his expatriation in Europe. Esther's extended depiction of the sufferings of contemporary Jewry, though interesting in itself, seems extraneous to the novel and mars its unity.

Having witnessed savagery against Jews in her native Morocco, Esther now devotes her mature years to assisting Jews in trouble, especially in Eastern Europe, where counter revolutionaries, fighting against the Bolsheviks, have slaughtered Jews in a manner anticipating Hitler. Esther mirrors Lewisohn's acute sense of the precarious state of Jewry in Europe and other areas; she foreshadows Arthur Levy's mission among Jews at the end of *The Island Within* (1928). Esther expresses as well Lewisohn's fear that the temptations of assimilation in America will deaden American Jews to their identity. Despite her affection for Austin, she will not marry him because of religious barriers. She also affirms her belief in companionate marriages, blending incongruously Lewisohn's still-maintained liberalism in the sexual arena and his increasing concern for the survival of Jewish values. This contradiction of ideas will remain with Lewisohn into the 1930s. Carrying an enormous ideological burden, Esther remains an unconvincing figure.

Austin, finally, presumably matured as a result of his discussions with Esther and warned by her of the dangers of deracination, returns to America to confront American realities. After marrying a girl of his own kind and class, he devotes himself to the Naturalistic novel, shorn of the English and genteel tradition. In a review of *Roman Summer* in the *London Daily Telegraph* (September 16, 1930), J. A. T. Lloyd makes this interesting comment: "It is a distinct variation from the only too familiar novel which presents the reactions of a young Puritan from the Middle West to the lure of Europe. In such works the Puritan returns to his native country usually gloriously amoral....John Austin, in this book, goes through no such transformation during his first visit to Rome...." Austin's eagerness to return home reflects the fact that, though Lewisohn lived abroad for a decade, his was not a voluntary exile, like Gertrude Stein's or Hemingway's; he lived in Europe because he felt he had been driven there.

Contemporary reviews of *Stephen Escott* (1930) criticized it as more thesis than novel. One can more properly say that it has too many theses. The book brings together a cluster of ideas and attitudes that make for an unwieldy whole. The jumble of themes in this novel reflect, possibly, unresolved dilemmas in Lewisohn's own make-up at that time.

The first theme emerges from Stephen Escott's gradual emancipation from American sexual Puritanism. The first-person narrator, Escott grows up in a New England town, in an oppressive household. His father suffers sexual frustrations; his mother, sexual repression. Inculcated in the genteel tradition, which his university only confirms, Stephen is shocked when, after his mother's death, his father moves to Boston to live with a "frowzy Irish woman." The woman seems below his father's social and educational level, but seems to fulfill his sexual and domestic needs.

Stephen, following in his father's footsteps, meets in college Dorothy Johnson, a pretty, prim, somewhat bigoted young lady. Their marriage remains passionless and childless; after thirteen years Dorothy dies, and Stephen in due course commences an affair with Beatrice Loth, a relationship more of lust than of love.

Beatrice is another of the author's snakelike, modern, "liberated" women. This relationship, also, proves unsatisfactory.

Reflecting on his life at a later point, Stephen says: "I married the first nice girl that would have me because of my hunger for sex and the satisfaction of my starved sexual self-esteem—couldn't wait any longer."[16] Of Beatrice Loth he says: "She's the rebellious type gone mad."[17] *Stephen Escott* defends genuine marital harmony without sexual repressions and attacks sexual experiment for its own sake.

A second strand in the novel concerns Paul Glover, a talented poet who lives in Greenwich Village and is married to Janet Reese. Glover has invested his love for his wife with an idealistic ardor and cannot accept her infidelity with Jasper Harris, a novelist and a casual philanderer. Glover slays Harris; his trial is declared a mistrial as a result of a hung jury. He is to fall at Belleau Wood, a death that is both punishment and redemption. Earlier, Glover delivers long, undramatized discourses explaining his homicide, with which Escott, one of his lawyers, seems to sympathize. Glover states he overvalued Janet as love-object, in the tradition of chivalry and courtly love. The whole episode displays Lewisohn's continued involvement in the opposite yet complementary acts of martyrdom and murder in matters of marital breakdown.

A third theme concerns itself with the one happy marriage in the novel. David Sampson, the brilliant young Jew who is Escott's law partner, and his wife Ruth enjoy a fulfilled non-puritanical marriage in which sex is accepted as a norm and a wife is content with her position as homemaker. As in *Roman Summer*, the Jew is here used as one who teaches lessons to the average American.

The novel is too preachy, talkative, and prone to undue generalization. Though it sold well and made best-seller lists, it deserved the unfriendly reviews it received. Thyra Samter Winslow, in the *New York Times*, wrote: "This book lacks unity, as we usually consider fictional unity, and it is as much a treatise on sex in relation to today's marriages as it is a novel."[18] The *Toledo Times* (March 10, 1931) stated: "His ideal woman, one gathers, is she who never forgets her feminine role and who makes no attempt to meet a man on his own ground and in his own intellectual field." Jonathan Daniels, in the *Saturday Review of Literature* (March 15, 1930), stated: "In Mr. Lewisohn's book the only successful marriage is one among people whose racial heritage and tradition of love and marriage keep them apart from the conventional American attitude."[19] Daniels found Lewisohn's arguments for the special value of Jewish marriage more sentimental than convincing. Frederick J. Hoffman has some praise for the novel in his *Freudianism and the Literary Mind:* it employs "psychoanalysis, not always subtly, but frequently with effectiveness." It "deals with the problem of marital unhappiness and its psychological implications."[20]

Certain patterns recur in these early novels: the unwary youth, raised in puritanical surroundings, trapped into an unhappy marriage; the need for sexual harmony in marriage; the promotion of such social and cultural circumstances as would produce such harmony.

The Golden Vase and *Altar in the Fields:* The Eternal Female

The Golden Vase (1931) is a short novel, which Lewisohn overestimated later as the pinnacle of his fiction. Actually, it is slight in content, though well organized, and tending, as was Lewisohn's frequent habit, to rely too heavily on exposition and not enough on dramatization. The novel has biographical interest as a defense of his merits at a time, after the success of *Up Stream, The Case of Mr. Crump,* and *The Island Within,* when his reputation was declining. *Mid-Channel* and *Stephen Escott* lessened the esteem in which Lewisohn had been held.

The protagonist, the novelist John Ridgevale—a genteel throwback to Henry James's portraits of the novelist and an anglicized version of Lewisohn himself—has been accused of lacking humor and of writing novels that are not novels. That Lewisohn had no humor and took himself too seriously was a critical truism in the thirties.[31] Ridgevale sums up his critics as follows: "If only, these people wrote, Ridgevale had any sense of humor, and the implication was that then, above all, he would see and perhaps avoid his own absurdity. And this absurdity, they pointed out explicitly enough, consisted of the portentous seriousness with which he took himself in his gigantic egoism...."[22] This criticism of Ridgevale-Lewisohn was valid. True, in his two best novels, humor of a sort is not lacking: *The Case of Mr. Crump* has grotesque touches, and *The Island Within* is filled with an effective dramatic irony, of men caught up and destroyed by their own devices. But, in the whole corpus of Lewisohn's work, one feels the lack of a certain self-scepticism. He took himself too seriously and his fiction not seriously enough.

Ridgevale bears the criticism and thinks his work has a redeeming virtue: "He had no humor. Well and good. Neither had Milton. He had—this was the revolutionary element in his works—he had celebrated the creative Eros."[23] With such assumptions of the prophet's mantle, Lewisohn merely compounded the complaints of humorlessness lodged against him.

Ridgevale is unhappily married to a Ph. D., a bluestocking who thinks creativity ceased in the seventeenth century. In Europe, while vacationing alone at a seaside resort, the novelist meets a young and beautiful admirer, Lisl Schönbrunn, a translator of his work. Their relationship is not consummated; Ridgevale feels he is too old for her and that she deserves a better destiny as wife and mother. The reader is unsure whether to praise him for his good sense or to accuse him, as the celebrator of the "creative Eros," of cowardice. In any event, Ridgevale sends the young lady as a parting gift a symbolic golden vase, an ancient terra-cotta vase he has plated with gold. Like Keats's Grecian urn, it depicts love and wholeness. The reader might ask: does one gold-plate ancient vases, gild the real thing?

Lewisohn explicitly explains his idea of the "creative Eros" at the end of the novel, relating it to the writings of Freud. The eternal female, the source of love, procreation, and infantile security, is also the source of art. Though he has lost Lisl, the novelist can renew his art: "He had had his vision—he had seen a woman dancing on the shore of the sea."[24]

An Altar in the Fields (1934) is not a good novel; its characters are lifeless and the temperature tepid; but it is intelligent and well organized. Dick Belden, from the Midwest, and Rose Trizevant, from Queenshaven—two areas Lewisohn knew about—are representative Manhattanites in the post-World-War-I generation. Both are in revolt against their puritanical upbringing and have a reasonably emancipated courtship and marriage.

Dick, closer to the author's sympathy, is the more conservative. He rejects the idea of complete sexual freedom. For him, "The new freedoms of contact and intercourse, the new unhindered companionships, the immensely greater social accessibility of women did not deepen or even promote a friendliness of the heart."[25] On the other hand, he did not want to return to the stodginess of his parents' way of life: "Hadn't he seen and known the stale, airless, lifeless marriages—the unspeakable homes of his adolescence and earlier youth? Didn't he remember the scraggy or icily portly women, grim with what they called morality, with unrelenting harpy-claws in the bitter-mouthed and furtively bawdy-tongued men whom they so relentlessly managed?" (*AF*, 53).

In contrast to Dick, Rose has a "more pliant and adventurous spirit." She is restive under the constraints of marriage, and, in seeking to develop as an actress, she rejects the idea of motherhood. "She withdrew her soul from her husband; she built about herself defenses against life" (*AF*, 127). After some years, however, of pursuing pleasures, of living in Europe, and of various professional misadventures, the Beldens—affected by a Jewish doctor who teaches them the need for religion and a renewed dedication—return to lasting verities. Dick buys a farm in New England and Rose becomes pregnant. By a tortuous route Lewisohn has his two characters accept his advocacy of wedded love and the assumption of responsibility. *An Altar in the Fields* is Lewisohn's belated answer to the Jazz Age.

Last Novels of Love and Marriage

Lewisohn's last three novels of love and marriage, spanning twenty years, show exhaustion. He had nothing new to add to what he had already said, and his issues did not seem relevant in periods of drastic social and economic change. His formative years, after all, roughly coincided with Sherwood Anderson's and Floyd Dell's; the battle against Puritanism and repression had been won; even Lewisohn's conservative modifications broke no new ground.

For Ever Wilt Thou Love (1939) can qualify as his worst novel. A group of married couples and their friends, with Mark Clement, an architect trying to maintain his artistic standards, as the dominating figure, discuss their sexual and marital enterprises in a stagy, unlikely way. They reveal intimate secrets without restraint and preach interminably. Clement, unhappily married to a frigid, yet flirtatious wife and disappointed in an extramarital, unfulfilled love with a girl too good to be true, philosophizes: "...all love is tragic. Love without the social sanctions is an outcast; it has no place in space and time; its wings are lamed by the tyranny of society even in the minds of the freest; and love within the sanctions of society is doomed to the attritions of the world. It dies."[26] The novel reflects an unusual bitterness, written after the end of Lewisohn's alliance with Thelma Spear and before his marriage to Edna Hanley. Even the kindly Carl Van Doren and Maurice Samuel, both of whom were friends, disapproved of *For Ever Wilt Thou Love*.[27]

Anniversary (1948) begins promisingly. Stressing the repressive climate of the small New England town—suggested, perhaps, by Burlington, Vermont, where Lewisohn and Thelma Spear lived after returning to the United States—it tells its story from the shifting points of view of the different characters. The first storytellers are individual townspeople, and Lewisohn thus can build up "naturalistic" effects—as with the Earnharts in *Roman Summer*—which he can do well. One regrets he did not explore the "naturalistic" approach more often. The townspeople are handled skillfully when they are center-stage.

Unfortunately, the second half of the novel is a fictional disaster, with the introduction of Anthony Foulk, an anthropologist, who, as the author's mouthpiece, delivers tedious lectures on American mores. The story records the liberation of Joy Munson from the suffocating perspectives of her town, her two bad marriages, and her eventual happiness with Foulk. If *An Altar of the Fields* chronicles the failures of an uprooted freedom, *Anniversary* swings Lewisohn's pendulum to the other side, the need for release from narrow-mindedness, hypocrisy, and excessive propriety.

In a Summer Season (1955) is a headless horseman of a novel, in which Lewisohn attempts uncertainly to confront various problems on the horizon: suburban infidelities, rebellious youth, Greenwich Village leftism. His targets are communism, excessive alimony demands, cold-hearted wives, the weakening of bourgeois values. Felix, the main character, laments the loss of a dream love. The hero is a Saul-Bellow-like figure, a confused man trying to keep his balance on the tightrope of modern life, but what emerges in the novel is confusion rather than a picture of confusion. Ultimately, Felix expresses a longing for the faith of his fathers: "Faith, some kind of faith, a sufficient faith—that ultimate point from which a rational life can proceed to be lived...."[28]

In only one novel of this group, *The Case of Mr. Crump,* does Lewisohn's narrative power, sense of form, and grasp of detail overbalance his inclination to wander outside the proper frame of fiction. Certain novels after *Mr. Crump* are intermittently successful: *Roman Summer, Stephen Escott, The Golden Vase.* In his outlook on love and marriage one notes certain analogies to Milton, in direction if not in power. Like Milton, Lewisohn advocates an easing of divorce laws, a linking of romance and marriage ("Hail, Wedded Love"), a misogyny directed against ambitious women, and an insistence that a woman's role is to lend support to her husband and to bear children. Striking an anti-Puritan pose, Lewisohn reminds the reader of one of the greatest Puritans in literature.

For Lewisohn's many unhappy male protagonists, a vision of a perfect, but unattainable love is present. In his later novels Jewish figures—Esther Azancort; David Sampson; Dr. Weyl in *An Altar in the Fields;* Jerome Goodman, the lawyer in *In a Summer Season*—serve as exemplary models. In these novels Lewisohn mixes romantic idealism, a naturalistic rebellion against puritanical repression, and a longing for an untroubled, but sexually satisfying domesticity.

Chapter Three
Novels of Jewish Content

Lewisohn wrote five novels of primarily Jewish content: *The Island Within, The Last Days of Shylock, Renegade, Breathe Upon These,* and *Trumpet of Jubilee,* as well as a collection of novellas: *This People.* Although these works are uneven in quality, they achieve a greater degree of artistic success than his non-Jewish novels. *The Island Within* is the best of this group, a work very different in kind from *The Case of Mr. Crump,* the best of his novels of love and marriage. *The Last Days of Shylock* and *Renegade* show an unsuspected skill—as do portions of *The Island Within*—in re-creating distant historical periods and places. *Renegade,* indeed, is still a readable, and sometimes exciting, historical novel. One novella, "Writ of Divorcement," is superior; a second, "Bolshevik," has an effective macabre quality. In addition to demonstrating an historical sense, the novels of this group show a greater awareness of current international trends than do his novels of love and marriage.

The Jewish figures appearing in his "American" novels are wooden and stereotyped. The Sampsons in *Stephen Escott,* Dr. Weyl in *An Altar in the Fields,* Esther Azancot in *Roman Summer,* and Goodman in *In a Summer Season* all serve as father-figures, confessors, and apostles to the Gentiles— something like the Jewish figures in Disraeli's novels. But the Jewish figures in Lewisohn's "Jewish" novels perform among their peers; therefore, they are less stilted, more problematic, and interesting.

The main theme in Lewisohn's Jewish fiction is the self-destruction wrought by the loss of one's religious identity. The process of assimilation turns back on itself, breeds internal division, and culminates in despair, sometimes even in suicide. On the other hand, identifying with one's people brings contentment and purpose.

Apparently, the psychic wounds Lewisohn had suffered—the rejection he felt he had suffered at Columbia University; the years of unhappy marriage and the prolonged legal entanglements thereafter; the ten years of expatriation; the difficulties of getting books that might offend published—left him with an acute sense of displacement. Perhaps he had brought some sense of alienation with him from Charleston. The hostility these problems bred contributed to his fascination with murder and suicide. They also compelled the search for an ordered structure of values that could accommodate him; all this might explain the fervor of his return to Judaism. Jews, too, had maintained their faith during a history of isolation and martyrdom, both of which he felt ingrained in himself.

But the return to a traditional structure of values did not rise solely from his own needs. The anti-Semitism apparent to him in Europe and the Near East reveals itself in *Israel*; he early saw the looming danger of Nazism. The issues of Jewish identity are more than personal. Lewisohn's *volte-face* still stands as a significant achievement, reminding American Jewish writers—often pulled in different directions—of the "island within," of a viable heritage that could not be sensibly ignored. Harold U. Ribalow writes: "...the probems limned by Lewisohn in the pre-Hitler days have not entirely disappeared. The Jew has come a long way since *The Island Within* ... but not all the way. The conflict of the generations, the problem of intermarriage, the probing for identity and self-esteem—these issues are still with us."[1]

The Island Within: The Key Novel

Like *The Case of Mr. Crump*, although not autobiographical, *The Island Within* (1928) is more concrete in content than argumentative. It also has an economy of style found in Lewisohn at his best. True, Lewisohn prefaces his chapters with brief essays, but they are succinct and aphoristic, and do not interrupt the flow of his narrative.

In a manner similar to other sagas of immigrant families, the author begins by recording the history of the ancestors of his hero, Arthur Levy, in Poland and Germany. He employs careful historical detail and a consummate irony. In 1840, in Vilna, Reb Mendel earns a precarious livelihood as a *malamed* ("Hebrew teacher"). Spiritually dry of heart, he is attracted to the new learning of the emancipated, the *Maskilim* ("the Enlightened"). After a while, he leaves his calling to work for the distiller Chaim Bratzlawer, a rich, influential, somewhat assimilated, and devious Jew. Mendel makes a better living, but his wife, Braine, is embittered at his transformation. Mendel himself misses his past scholarly study, and his internal conflict breaks him. At the moment of his death he recites the *Schema*, Israel's essential prayer ("Hear, Oh Israel! There is only one God; the Lord God is one"). Braine, anticipating her son's drift toward assimilation, leaves for Palestine—a rather rare exodus in those days.

Their son, Efrem, works for Bratzlawer, too, marries his employer's youngest daughter, Hannah, and in 1850 proceeds to Germany to manufacture kümmel wine. He takes as his last name Levi (later Levy) and maintains an Orthodox home, though German is spoken there, not Yiddish.

Continuing the drift toward assimilation, his older son, Tobias, goes to a *gymnasium* and then, in 1869, to the University of Königsberg. Tobias marries into the Burghammer family, a clan of wealthy converted Jews, and undergoes Christian baptism himself. He becomes the distinguished jurist Theodore Burghammer. In 1917 his older son is killed in the war; nevertheless, in Germany's hour of defeat, rioting crowds storm his doors denouncing Jews. Tobias-Theodore, now an old man, impulsively cries out in a loud voice words he had not heard for fifty years: "Schema Yisrael!" ("Hear, O Israel!"). The bankruptcy of assimilation reveals itself here in Germany, as it will for Arthur Levy in America. This German section in *The Island Within* contrasts with the pro-German attitudes manifested in Lewisohn's critical writings during World War I.

Jacob, the youngest of Efrem's children, had seduced a young Gentile girl and had been forced to emigrate to America. There he mends his scapegrace ways and gradually succeeds in business as a founder of a furniture house, Goldmann and Levy. He is married by a Reformed rabbi to Gertrude Oberwater, an American by birth and "American" in outlook. Their home, on the upper West Side of Manhattan, has no visible symbols of religion, though Jacob has occasional religious impulses. Arthur, their son, born in 1893, assumes the central role in the novel; he has no religious training, but is reminded of the fact that he is Jewish by occasional events in his childhood; in one, he is subjected to anti-Semitic taunts by a gang of rowdies.

The Goldmann and Levy children think they are typically American, though they are sheltered in the strictly German-Jewish circle in which they are brought up. Joe Goldmann, the son of Jacob's partner, enters Columbia University with Arthur in 1910. Joe is a Marxist; Arthur, like Lewisohn, is not interested in Marx, but prefers the study of psychology, particularly of Freud and Rank. The Jewish students at Columbia try to disappear into the academic camouflage, to act exactly the same as the Christian students. Arthur reflects: "Was not some, at least, of the well-bred quietude which commended him to his gentile friends the result of a definite discipline and the shadow of a hidden shame?" Arthur finds the poorer Russian Jews on the lower East Side alien and repulsive. In one of his short prefatory essays Lewisohn excoriates the protective mimicry of modern Jews: "Can the Jewish imagination live permanently and gladly as though it shared in historic experiences which, in fact, Jews watched from without as outcasts and martyrs?"[2]

Arthur becomes a psychiatrist, and his experience in hospital wards leads him to believe that insanity, deriving often from flights from reality, resembles the mechanism of the Jewish anti-Jewish complex. His Jewish friends and associates suffer from this malaise: "The Freefields, Eugene Adams, Joe Goldmann, his brother Victor—they were all in flight from a disagreeable reality whether their flight was toward pomp and patriotism or toward techniques of life which would insure gentile society or toward dreams of world-revolution which would set the crooked straight, or merely toward a cloud of arrogant disputatiousness..." (*IW*, 187). His discoveries as a psychiatrist make him identify more as a Jew.

Nevertheless, he falls in love with the non-Jewish Elizabeth Knight, who represents a compound of two kinds of American woman whom Lewisohn deplores. She combines the puritanical and the "liberated" woman. She had suffered an unhappy upbringing in a puritanical setting and had carried over many of its attitudes into the laxer New York environment of her young womanhood. She is a parson's daughter turned feminist. She will appear again as Rose Trezivant in *An Altar in the Fields* (1934), the confused New York girl of the 1920s. Just as Lewisohn introduces the Jew as contrast and example in his novels of non-Jewish Americans, so here he incorporates one of his critical characterizations of American women.

At the time Arthur meets Elizabeth, "Her virginity was evidently an ache to her, an ache at least as much of the mind as of the body, and she resisted this troubling wound and lack at the core of her and had cultivated a harsh, almost petulant hostility to men" (*IW*, 187). Even after they became lovers, "Her ultimate inhibitions were never quite broken down." When Elizabeth becomes pregnant, she resists the fact that they now will be married, for then her role would be one of "slave and nurse." Arthur tries to convey the idea to her that motherhood is normal, but Elizabeth rejects the lesson. She is "the eternal Diana, maiden and huntress." Arthur has less success as teacher than Dr. Weyl does with the Beldens (*An Altar in the Fields*).

The marriage breaks down as he becomes increasingly Jewish in outlook and she is trapped in the dilemmas of an American upbringing. Arthur accepts Lewisohn's concept of Jewish marriage, in which the woman embodies a *tertium quid* between subjection and emancipation. As Elizabeth develops into a successful writer, she becomes more detached from her role as wife, mother, and in-law. As Arthur sees it, Elizabeth has denied her natural instincts, and a separation finally ensues.

Observing his Jewish friends and associates, Arthur notes a paradox. Though they all, in different ways, have put aside their Jewishness, they feel more comfortable and accepted in the company of other Jews. He himself in his practice has mostly Jewish patients; Victor Goldmann, a successful architect and a cynic about religion, builds temples for Jewish clients; Joe Goldmann, a lawyer, has an office full of Jewish clients, but "espouses world revolution and [is] always in love with some blond Gentile girl...." (*IW*, 210). Arthur's friends flee reality; finally, in self-disgust, Victor commits suicide.[3]

Arthur takes employment in a Jewish hospital and feels at home. He contemplates: "Here, among Jews, one could be most human, most personal, least herd-minded—least torn between the instincts of one herd and those of another ..." (*IW*, 305). He need not live in a continued effort to evade stereotypes of Jews among non-Jews. In the hospital he meets Reb Hacohen, a *chassid*, who reveals that he is a relative of Levy's; both are direct descendants of Reb Mendel and Braine, with whom the novel began. Arthur consents to his cousin's suggestion that he join a commission to investigate the plight of Jews in Rumania. The pattern of flight and separation follows somewhat a novel Lewisohn wrote five years earlier, *Don Juan*.

Although *The Island Within* begins as a saga of emigration toward the West and later concentrates on Arthur's marital difficulties, its basic theme provides sufficient unity. The thesis itself is projected forthrightly.

Contemporary reviewers were impressed. Bertrand Russell in the *Foreword* (May 13, 1928), before proceeding to a long discourse on Jewish-Christian relations, praised the novel. Granville Hicks in the *Nation* called it "the most nearly perfect thesis novel of our generation."[4] Irwin Edman in the *Menorah Journal* wrote: "Its problem, that of the adjustment of the honest and sensitive young Jew to Judaism, the island within, and to the ocean of alien culture in which that island is set, is one in which Mr. Lewisohn has, with less mellowness, earlier given expression... he has written a tender, poetical, lucid, and passionate book. Any American Jew reading it will recognize it as a true tale about ourselves."[5]

Some reviewers raised cavils. Bernard de Voto, in the *Saturday Review of Literature* (May 5, 1928), thought the novel was distinguished but lost power because of its epic scope; the story of Arthur Levy does not dominate as it should.[6] But one can argue against de Voto that Arthur's story achieves greater dimension as part of a larger framework. Some readers thought Lewisohn unfair to Elizabeth, not allowing her to relate her point of view. Johan Smertenko raises an interesting point: "...though this reviewer is in complete accord with Lewisohn's premise that at present a self-respecting Jew cannot be assimilated in America, he must confess that the proof in this novel is not altogether convincing. Arthur breaks with Elizabeth Knight...not through any conflict of Jewish and American life-modes but basically because Arthur is a nineteenth-century bourgeois and seeks a Victorian domesticity...whereas Elizabeth is a member of the 'younger generation,' hectically liberated, slightly undersexed, and completely irreligious."[7] Lewisohn saw the conflict between Elizabeth and Arthur as one between American and Jewish modes. But the reader might ask: Are these modes inevitably so antagonistic? Is the sexual repression displayed in Elizabeth universally woven into the fabric of American life?

The Island Within sold very well at time of publication and has proved the most durable of Lewisohn's fiction in terms of publication history. It appeared as a Modern Library edition for some years and has recently been reprinted by the Jewish Publication Society. Among others, Dr. Rueben Abel, Dean of Humanities for the New School in New York, has referred in conversation to the strong effect the novel had on publication in Jewish student and literary circles. Lewisohn was the first American-Jewish man of letters to advocate a return to the "island within"; the book had shock value.[8]

The Last Days of Shylock: History as Novel

The Last Days of Shylock (1931), which appeared with illustrations by Arthur Szyk, marked a departure for Lewisohn. Hitherto concerned essentially with the contemporary scene, he here re-creates Shakespeare's Shylock and, placing him in historical perspective, attempts to make Shakespeare's villain more comprehensible and worthy of vindication.

It is a work of mixed merit. Reflecting the author's research into Jewish history during the Renaissance, the novel has descriptive power, seen earlier in *Israel* and *Cities and Men* but not in Lewisohn's fiction. It weaves a tapestry of Mediterranean settings; indeed, its picture of Palestine in Shakespeare's time qualifies as a tour de force. Also, the conception of Shylock is penetrating. Cold and bitter because of his past sufferings and the sufferings of his race, he is also propelled by religious devotion, by a sense of justice, and by enterprise and vigor. Interestingly, in order to broaden the historical landscape, Lewisohn does not dwell upon the events in *The Merchant of Venice*. Shylock looks back upon his earlier life elsewhere and, in vigorous old age, lives in different places for years after leaving Venice as exile. His forced conversion, which he quickly sheds, is only a low point in his checkered and largely useful career.

The weakness of the book in its lack of vitality, due to a lack of dominant *action* in Aristotle's phrase, of *fable* in Samuel Johnson's. Lewisohn seems so intent on background that there is no foreground. Shylock pushes Venetian events out of mind, but nothing central replaces them. The reader cannot grasp a story. Nor does the novel qualify as successfully picaresque since no episodes are engrossing enough to compensate for its lack of central focus. For all Lewisohn's historical thoroughness, descriptive skills, polished style, and sufficient objectivity in viewing Shylock, the novel does not come off.

It begins immediately after Shylock's trial, the moment of defeat. Shylock reflects that he would not have exacted the pound of flesh: "For who in all the world had ever heard of the legality of a contract which did not render legal the means of carrying out its provisions? ... His knife would not have gone very deeply into the bosom of his adversary."[9] He feels most deeply the apostasy of his daughter, Jessica.

Shylock contemplates his past: "He was not of those who could forget. Images once imprinted upon his mind remained; injustices gnawed at his soul; cruel and importunate memories pursued him into the very house of prayer."[10] He remembers past oppression, humiliation, and merciless slayings, including that of his father when Shylock was seventeen. The Inquisition and expulsion of Jews from their native lands are events recent enough to be engraved in his thoughts. He recalls the Christian invasion of Tunis in 1535 and the slaughter of Moslems and Jews that followed. The Jews surviving the massacre were sold into slavery.

Although Shylock grew in wealth as a moneylender in Venice, his chief activity and interest, in Lewisohn's conception, was to serve as Venetian agent for the Houses of Mendes and Nasi, families engaged in securing the welfare of Jews in various countries. These houses were the equivalent in those times of modern congresses and committees. Shylock performed many services in Venice and abroad as an envoy for Donna Grazia of the House of Nasi and later for her son Joseph.

After his baptism, which he disregards as an externally imposed allegiance, Shylock flees Venice to join Joseph Nasi, now the treasurer of the Turkish Sultan, Suleiman, and later of the Sultan's son and successor, Selim. The intrigues at the court render Joseph's position uneasy. Joseph requests and is granted the ruined city of Tiberias and seven wrecked villages in Palestine as places of refuge for outcast Hebrews. Thus Lewisohn introduces the Zionist idea, to which he was strongly committed, into the novel. Shylock, as Joseph's emissary to Palestine, witnesses the tribulations of early Hebrew pioneers and the enmities of Jews and Arabs—not a recent phenomenon. Shylock's adventures in Palestine make up the most interesting section of the novel.

Serving as paymaster on an expedition to Cyprus, in which the Turks defeat the Venetians, Shylock meets his daughter Jessica again, a refugee from Venice. Now the mother of three children, she has fallen out with Lorenzo, who has treated her cruelly and berated her as a Jewess. Shylock and Jessica are reconciled, and in the company of his daughter and his grandchildren Shylock enjoys peace in his last days.

Jewish leaders had great praise for *Shylock*. In a letter Rabbi Louis Finkelstein, for many years Chancellor of the Jewish Theological Seminary, while correcting two minor mistakes, wrote: "the book is, to my mind, the finest defense of the medieval Jew against the calumnies usually heaped against him, and the best introduction."[11] A letter from Rabbi Stephen S. Wise (February 9, 1931) reads: "Dear Lewisohn, you have done a great book. It will live in Jewish history...." Maurice Samuel in the New York *Jewish Tribune* (January 3, 1931) commended its "grave, heavily tapestried pages," its craftsmanship, and measured responsibility. He encouraged Lewisohn to continue a series of such novels.

Literary reviewers were more critical. Granville Hicks in the *Nation* did not find that the author resolved the problem of Shakespeare's vengeful Shylock with his own more sympathetic picture.[12] Florence Haxton Britten granted some beautiful writing, but wrote that "the stream as a whole is turgid, flows slowly...."[13]

The Last Days of Shylock was a Book-of-the-Month selection, but was finally remaindered.

This People: Modern False Lights

This People, a collection of five novellas (1933), delineates the conflicts of modern Jews tempted by alternative lifestyles.

The most important story is "Writ of Divorcement," a novella unfortunately forgotten, but included by Harold U. Ribalow in his anthology *The Chosen* (1959). It is an interesting variation of *The Island Within.* This time the marital unhappiness at the core of the work does not stem from an intermarriage but between two of the same faith, with Myrtle Kessler the source of the difficulty as a Jewish girl trying to escape her Jewishness. This modern, "emancipated" young woman, a Vassar graduate, has the same problems of frigidity as did Elizabeth Knight, the offspring of puritanical parents. Lewisohn thus corrects the impression left in *The Island Within* of too broadly generalizing about Jewish modes as against "American" modes.

The first-person narrator, whose father is a rabbi of German origin, tells the story in somewhat documentary fashion, interweaving comment and narrative in a manner reminiscent of Dostoevsky. Editorial comment when skillfully done by a first-person narrator is somehow less bothersome than when delivered by a novelist putting on his lecturer's robes. The rabbi's home has a beautiful spirit, synthesizing the religious and the secular. But the youth, later an architect, succumbs to modern trends; he undergoes his period of rebellious youth. He does not fully heed the warnings of his father that sex is not a free activity but an aspect of wholesome family life: "I shall not say that I permitted myself to be wholly convinced by my father's discourse; had I permitted myself to be convinced I would never have married Myrtle Kessler, nor suffered so nor caused her so to suffer...."[14]

Myrtle, an unloving wife, shrinks from his advances. Her coldness proceeds from her confusion, her self-hatred, her turning away from all that is Jewish. "She has in her subconscious, at least, identified passions both of mind and body as Jewish...."[15] The narrator perceives his father's wisdom, and Myrtle and he are eventually divorced.

The story, although well paced and with mounting suspense, suffers from riding its theme too hard. It would benefit from greater subtlety. Nevertheless, it retains the reader's interest and makes him feel the witness of a real experience.

The second most interesting story is the macabre "Bolshevik," which the author in correspondence called a "hard, cold, bitter story." Masha, a Jewish prostitute, loves Jan Zorn, who loves no one. A dedicated Communist, he was born a very poor Jew, named Isaac Goldfarb, in Eastern Europe. As a youth filled with self-hatred and attracted to Polish peasant girls who reject him, he is led to radicalism through sexual deprivation and sterility of purpose. He is a Bolshevik through loneliness and deracination. Finally, he is killed by youthful Nazis in Germany because he is both a Communist and a Jew. His death wish, his desire for self-annihilation, is detected in his face after death: "They had stricken him in the back. Upon his unhurt face was an expression of relaxation, almost of ecstasy." Of "Bolshevik," John J. Smertenko wrote: "[It] gleams like an evil cat's eye. Here is perversity of spirit...."[16] The story combines Lewisohn's faith in Judaism, his early antipathy to Nazism, his psychological approach to character, and his rigid non-Marxist posture.

The other three stories are of lesser interest. "The Saint" has the nostalgic realism of an Edith Wharton story. Indeed, it calls to mind "False Dawn" of her Old New York series, though without a commensurate power. At the turn of the century a well-to-do Jewish family but devoid of religious feelings, the Birnbaums live on the upper West Side in Manhattan. A son, Leon, is inexplicably attracted to religious orthodoxy. Leon marries, creates a religious household, and embodies all the attitudes Lewisohn favors, including anti-Communism. At Leon's premature death he is called a *zaddik* ("saint") and one of the thirty-six unrecognized righteous men who hold up the world. The story is concerned with the conflict of assimilation and identification; it is neatly done, but not compelling.

"The Romantic" is unlikely melodrama. The Baron, of Jewish descent but whose father has converted to Catholicism, returns to his native land, Carpathia, as a political emigré. He has been given a promise of safe conduct, but is slain with the contrivance of the authorities because he is a Jew. The story makes little sense, but, once more, displays the author's keen awareness of the totalitarian bent toward genocide.

The fifth story, "By the Waters of Babylon," as the reviewer Mary Ross summarized, is "a 'faint legend' that the widowed Queen Esther and Mordecai returned and lived to see the city of Jerusalem rebuilt and the Temple a place of glory."[17] Like *The Last Days of Shylock,* the story is rich in local color but short on narrative; it, also, displays much research in Hebrew, German, and English sources.

This People was well received; two stories of this group still have interest and force.

Trumpet of Jubilee: Soon the Apocalypse

Lewisohn records in *Haven* his dismay at the small sales of *For Ever Wilt Thou Love* and *Trumpet of Jubilee* (1937). *Trumpet of Jubilee* is the better of the two novels, though it deserves only faint praise. Despite its title, the work is pessimistic, written on the brink of World War II. It projects events into the future. It scores points in its favor because of Lewisohn's vision of things to come: the death camps in Germany; the fall of France; the confrontation of the Russians and the Nazis; the near-destruction of the world (latent, one would say, in the promise of the atomic bomb). The predictions made in the novel have proven more true than false.

But *Trumpet of Jubilee* is marred by the grab-bag miscellany of its contents. It reads as though Lewisohn had assembled three or four different ideas for various novels and roughly joined them together. He begins with a framework of three men in conversation, each representing an important point of view: Peter Lang, the perennial Christian; Jehuda Brenner, the perennial Jew; and Andrew Saracen, the materialist and Communist. These are introduced in the Prologue but dropped as the novel continues.

Book I, "Burning World," set in Germany, deals with the Nazi destruction of ancient Jewish communities. In Frankfurt Dr. Kurt Weiss, a well-established Jewish lawyer, is gradually trapped and ultimately castrated and slain by a local Nazi group. Weiss, confident of his German citizenship, and his wife, Gina, immersed in Mozart and Beethoven, were slow to believe that Nazism was more than a passing phenomenon. After Weiss's death Gina and their son, Gabriel, flee to Paris and then to America.

The events of this First Book bear some similarities to Gerald Green's recent television scenario of *Holocaust*. Lewisohn—not alone to be sure—must be credited with foresight instead of hindsight. Apparently a pattern for fiction in dealing with Jews was set by 1937. "Burning World" in itself, with some expansion, would have constituted a whole novel, perhaps a better one than *Trumpet of Jubilee* as it now is.

Book II, "Apocalypse," traces Gabriel Weiss's growing up in America to become Lewisohn's paragon. The section is weak and sometimes ludicrous. It encompasses a period that extends beyond 1937. Gabriel is a lover, a poet influenced by Rilke, and a serious Jew. He has a maturing love affair with Elizabeth Warner, a beautiful and married Gentile; at one point in an idyllic vacation together, he states he cannot take part in some activity because the day is the Sabbath! A Lewisohn absurdity. He finds a job at the Jewish Junior College Unit of Ozark City—a strange example of Lewisohn' notion of an expanded cultural pluralism in the United States in the future. Gabriel finally enters into a happy marriage with Eve Israel, who bears the descriptive cognomen *par excellence.*

Some typical themes recur: Dr. Jacoby, the self-hating Jew, kills himself; Alan Jones is trapped by seduction into a marital nightmare; the American community is subjected to the author's attack on the grounds of prudery and materialism. At the end, the novel discourses on the great war to come. As the great battle is waged between Nazi Germany and the Soviet Union, America is drawn in. The few men who survive the ensuing apocalypse return to primitive myths and ancient religions; the history of the world will repeat itself.

Trumpet of Jubilee demonstrates the fact that pretty good prophecy does not necessarily make good fiction. Lewisohn reveals a sensitive and accurate response to international currents, with a properly bleak view of the world to come, mixed with a somewhat contradictory positive outlook on Jewish life to come. The book lacks design; the material overruns form or central theme.

Renegade: His Best Historical Novel

As Lewisohn was lamenting the poor reception of *For Ever Wilt Thou Love* and *Trumpet of Jubilee* (even American Jews, he complained, did not support the second), he was shaping his next novel, *Renegade* (1942). An historical novel, it treats of the Jewish community in France during the latter half of the eighteenth century, with an excursion into Poland at the end. It is marked by the author's usual careful research and his ability to describe and reconstruct. Lewisohn saw it as more than history; it is, he said, "a narrative bodying forth present and universal issues under the symbolisms of 1797–1770...."[18] *Renegade,* like nearly all his fiction of Jewish content, assumes the form of the hero's willful departure from the Jewish community and then his reflexive return.

Lewis Gannett of the *New York Tribune* (March 4, 1942) wrote that *Renegade* was the best of Lewisohn's recent fiction.

The *New York Times* reviewer praised the author's "penetrating mind" and "superb gifts as a storyteller."[19] Though his earlier historical novel was lifeless, this novel—perhaps in reaction to the earlier one—abounds in lively incident, sometimes to the point of melodrama and unlikely coincidence. But it is entertaining, a pleasant reading experience, without authorial intrusions. It presents Lewisohn's theme in palatable guise. Though a lesser work than *The Case of Mr. Crump* and *The Island Within,* it ranks with two stories in *This People* as his next best fiction.

The young, unmarried hero, Joshua (Josué) Vidal, has moved to Paris with his family from Avignon, where Sephardic Jews like himself had lived for generations. Influenced by Voltaire and Rousseau, Vidal longs to escape his Jewish confines and enter the larger world: "...that he in the Age of Reason and Humanity should dwell forever in the dark Jews' street and be cut off from the light and rumor of the world, was a thing unbearable and not to be thought of."[20]

His interest in the *philosophes* meets with no kindly response from his grandfather, a traditional sage and patriarch, or his father, a sharp, worldly man of affairs and banker. But their antagonism does not diminish his pleasure in the fact that "he, a Jew of Avignon who, until two years ago, had worn the yellow Jew's hat obligatory in the Papal county of Venaissin, could mingle with at least the half-world of the capital unnoticed, even admired."

At first sight, he falls in love with Marguerite de Saint-Florentin, a *comtesse* who has business dealings with his father. His passion for her will dominate his thinking and behavior for the rest of his life. Despite their differences in class and religion, "She became the vision of his days and his nights." Through the connivance of a renegade Jew, the somewhat sinister entrepreneur and go-between, Valdes, he meets Marguerite's husband, the Comte de Saint-Florentin, a braggart, fool, and would-be poet, much older than his wife. Led on by love and with sufficient wealth, Joshua seizes the opportunity, with Valdes's help, to "pass" as a young Christian nobleman and mingle in the set of the Saint-Florentins. Thus Joshua himself becomes a renegade Jew.

Marguerite reciprocates his affection. Originally a country girl, she had been forced to marry to relieve her family's financial difficulties. Vidal acquires power over the Comte by lending him money, for the Comte has dissipated most of his estate. Joshua reflects: "Ah, how right was the divine Jean-Jacques concerning the iniquity of the laws of an artificial society.... Was it not detestable enough that this fat pretentious coxcomb owned Marguerite both body and soul?.... he had to be bribed and pampered in addition."

Saint-Florentin pays lip service to the *philosophes,* but is basically interested in gratifying his appetites. He overlooks the attention Vidal pays his wife because he reaps financial benefits. Joshua is amazed that an aristocratic circle interested theoretically in the *philosophes* should be thoroughly corrupt in practice and entirely anti-Semitic.

Marguerite loves Vidal, but feels he is strange and mysterious. At one point, the Comte and Comtesse, Vidal, and the Comte's jealous and bitter mistress, Lisette, sojourn in the village of Dieu-Le-Fit. An interesting love-quadrangle emerges. Each is aware of the others' feelings, yet each is trapped in a seemingly insoluble dilemma. This section, chapter 5 of *Renegade*, is a high point in Lewisohn's fiction. The author handles the bizarre comedy expertly and completely rivets the reader's attention. The section displays both narrative mastery and character insights.

The knot is slashed when Lisette discovers and unveils the fact that Vidal is a Jew. After securing Marguerite against attack by settling upon her mortgages he has purchased upon Saint-Florentin's estate, Joshua returns to Paris and, reconciled to his Jewishness, tells his story to his grandfather. The old sage is surprisingly sympathetic and advises the youth to have patience, to be guilty of no act. The next decision must be Marguerite's, and the old man cites cases of conversion to Judaism in parallel circumstances.

Joshua becomes a messenger, an outside agent, for the Jewish community in Paris; he spends three years in Strasbourg, where he becomes acquainted with German Jewry and has unexpected meetings with Herder and Goethe, two of Lewisohn's perennial heroes.

The last part of *Renegade*, the most melodramatic, strains the reader's capacity to suspend disbelief. Joshua sets out for Warsaw, is impressed by leaders of the Polish *chassidim,* meets the legendary jester Ostropoler, sees anti-Semitism in loathsome forms, and is rescued from prison by Marguerite, now a widow. She converts, they marry, and they emigrate to the West Indies. Husband and wife serve as models of piety in Kingston, where Joshua dies in 1813. His wife, Ruth (neé Marguerite) becomes a princess of Israel.

Renegade bears surface resemblances to I. B. Singer's *The Slave* (1962), which also exalts love above considerations of class and caste, but lacks *The Slave's* delicacy and almost total objectivity. Nevertheless, *Renegade* reveals more of Lewisohn as an untrammeled storyteller than elsewhere. As a novel of adventure and intrigue in addition to thesis, it is still enjoyable.

Just a note on Lewisohn's last Jewish novel, *Breathe Upon These* (1944). The work seems tired and is easily forgotten, though concerned with moving materials.

The Burnetts are a typical upper-class American family; Ada feels her life is routine and empty and lacks the overt affection of her husband, Paul. Most of the novel covers a dinner visit of the Dorfsohns, Jewish refugees from Germany. Dorfsohn is Burnett's colleague in wartime scientific research. Dorfsohn relates to the Burnetts what is going on in Europe behind the battlelines— the concentration camps, ships bearing refugees going to Palestine and not gaining admittance, America's indifference. Presumably his narrative benefits the Burnetts by shaking them out of their deep freeze. Unfortunately, in light of the important subject matter, the reading is a chore.

Conclusion

The picture of Lewisohn that emerges from a reading of his Jewish fiction is that of an uneven and unpredictable novelist, sometimes firm in form but lacking moving content, sometimes lacking form but with an abundance of content. He is too often careless, writing for quick publication and indifferent to revision.

Nevertheless, his Jewish novels are superior as a whole to his novels of love and marriage. It may be argued that *The Case of Mr. Crump* is his masterwork, but his other novels of love and marriage rarely rise above mediocrity. Of the novels just considered, *The Island Within* is superior, and *Renegade* and two of the novellas in *This People* are good. These novels cover a broad historical spectrum, ranging from the Renaissance to almost the present, and can enlighten when not engrossing the reader. Just as recurring themes appear in his novels of love and marriage, so a recurrent theme appears in these—that the rewards of assimilation are short-lived, that deracination is self-destructive, and that one must retain or regain one's ethnic identity.

Examination convinces that Lewisohn did not lose his literary skills when he reverted strongly to Judaism. He remained, as ever, a writer with inconsistent success, with unexpected highs and lows.

Chapter Four

Lewisohn as Critic I: From Naturalism through Expressionism to Humanism

Carl Van Doren, a colleague of Lewisohn's on the *Nation* preferred Lewisohn as critic to Lewisohn as novelist. He wrote: "Disciplined by learning, his mind kept a Goethean serenity when he wrote about literature, however passionate his emotions. In his novels he seemed to be writing about emotions that seemed relatively new to him, and not quite mastered. A disciplined mind outlives the emotions that besiege it." Van Doren preferred those writings that displayed Lewisohn's "lucid mind" to those that revealed his troubled heart.[1]

One can agree with this proposition, provided he is allowed to except Lewisohn's two best novels. Though many of his novels, especially those of love and marriage, have no lasting merit—the thesis rendered threadbare and the material insufficiently dramatized, his critical writings, in various degrees, nearly all have value.

His early criticisms from the academy were clear, informative, and well expressed. His journalism for the *Nation* applied high standards to literature and drama, purgative without being small-spirited. His *Cities and Men* were his ripest studies, and in his relaxed moments in *Expression in America* he provided first-rate analyses. He is on weakest grounds when he is most combative, forgetting to keep "his eye on the object" (in Matthew Arnold's phrase) and letting the personal tensions of his novels enter into his critical writings. The best examples of this tendency are the anti-puritanical and Freudian sections of *Expression in America*. Lewisohn is at his best as a critic, which is often, when he is least tendentious.

Writing on German Literature:
the Creed of Flexible Naturalism

Lewisohn's first significant criticism rose from his work as teacher of German at Ohio State University. During that time he edited the dramatic works of Gerhart Hauptmann (seven volumes, 1912-1915, and two additional volumes subsequently, in the 1920s), an imposing task followed by *The Modern Drama* (1915), *The Spirit of Modern German Literature* (1916), and *The Poetry of Modern France* (1918). One distinction of these books is that they opened up areas of Continental literature scantily known to American readers. As Alfred Kazin wrote, "Before coming to the *Nation,* Lewisohn had done yeoman pioneer labor in adapting modern European literature to American criticism. ..."[2]

Reading through the volumes of plays of Gerhart Hauptmann (1862-1946) that Lewisohn edited from 1912 to 1915 is a pleasant enterprise. Hauptmann authorized the edition, and Lewisohn corresponded with him on troublesome points. Of the twenty-three plays included (Hauptmann, who lived through the era of Hitler, had done his best work by 1915), Lewisohn translated fifteen as well as two fragments; he felt free to revise and correct the other eight translations. His introductions to each volume are marked by editorial restraint, lucidity, and sober good sense. His comments encompass a knowledge of European drama ranging from the Greeks through Shakespeare, Calderon, and Grillparzer. The depth of his scholarship was always impressive, comparable to that of Paul Elmer More, Irving Babbitt, Van Wyck Brooks, and James Huneker.

Hauptmann, he writes, began in the naturalisic tradition that prevailed in German letters after the Franco-Prussian War, but soon transcended any doctrine of shallow positivism. The dramatist rose above the narrow views of scientism into the larger realms of tragedy. Though in his social plays the fates of his characters were determined by environment and though Hauptmann condemned "the injustice and inhumanity of the social order,"[3] he pleaded no causes and tried to convey a sense of the fullness of life. He attempted to show humanity in the round.

Lewisohn explains the difficulties of translating Hauptmann's dialectical usages. In the plays the Berlin populace spoke an "extraordinary degraded jargon" and the speech of Hauptmann's native Silesia was distinctly provincial. Lewisohn decided to employ in his translations a general but recognizable lower-class English, ignoring cockney or other distinctive English dialects, content to lose thereby a degree of accuracy or power, without introducing the greater evil of intrusive cultural traits foreign to Hauptmann's characters.

The German playwright, in his later career, shared the Neoromantic and Symbolist revolt in modern drama against Naturalism, and turned to legendary and Symbolic drama: "The poet thus becomes a seeker; he questions the ... quality of various ultimate values...."[4] All in all, Hauptmann's plays succeed "in presenting characters whose vital truth achieves the intellectual beauty and moral energy of great art."[5] Influenced by Hauptmann and other German writers, Lewisohn demonstrates for the first time the theory of a flexible Naturalism that constitutes one of the best components of his criticism. His edition in English remained standard for decades.

The Modern Drama (1915), written at Columbus, Ohio, followed upon his editing of Hauptmann. As a study of the modern Continental drama, it still has value; so knowledgeable an authority as Eric Bentley, in *The Playwright as Thinker,* called it "one of the better books on modern drama."[6]

The specific virtue of the book rests in Lewisohn's defense of the "modern" in modern drama when this literature was still a matter of controversy. Usually the "modern" theater was represented by contemporary critics as lacking the nobility of the traditional theater. Lewisohn undertakes his defense by releasing the drama from Aristotelian concepts. As Adolph Gillis in his study of Lewisohn aptly states:

The older drama ... concerned itself largely with depicting the transgression of the moral law by the individual and its vindication in the punishment of the transgressor ... whereas the modern drama ... 'denies the supremacy of any ethical criterion, social or religious, sweeps aside the conception of absolute guilt and the acquiescence in retributive justice as re-establishing the moral harmony of the world.' Thus the modern drama deprives man's will of the time-honored underpinning of a moral certitude, the breaking of which lends such poignant grandeur to the older play, and instead leaves him, a solitary soul, unsure of truth and justice anywhere in the universe yet 'crying out after reconciliation with an uncomprehended world...in which he must strive, if he would live at all, to be at home.'[7]

From the vantage point of today many of Lewisohn's judgments seem fallacious. To be sure, he recognizes Ibsen as the pioneer of modern drama, who overturned Aristotle's conceptions of tragedy. Ibsen, too, represented the paradigm of the modern dramatist, proceeding from Romanticism to Naturalism and then to Symbolism. But Lewisohn doesn't adequately recognize the merits of *The Wild Duck:* "*The Wild Duck* (1884) exhibits, not too clearly, or powerfully, a variety of characters corrupted by insufficient security of free self-hood."[8] He also calls Hedda Gabler "an ignoble egotist." Ibsen's one flawless masterpiece, for Lewisohn, is *Ghosts.* Finally, Lewisohn writes short-sightedly of the Norwegian dramatist: "I can think of no writer of equal rank in the history of literature so lacking in energy, in passion, or in charm" (*Drama,* 23).

Though he has high regard for Shaw, he makes the dubious statement (finding an echo in the English critic, William Archer) that "this remarkable writer is not, in the strictest sense, a creative artist at all..." (*Drama,* 201). Lewisohn dismisses Oscar Wilde's *The Importance of Being Earnest* as "mere farce." The foremost English dramatist, in his view, is John Galsworthy, whose plays in 1915 were generally overrated but have suffered the cruel compensation of being unfairly and totally neglected today. The book understandably does not mention Chekhov or Pirandello; the latter was not translated into English until the 1920s. But *The Modern Drama* is good on Henri Becque, August Strindberg, W. B. Yeats, Synge, and especially the German dramatists, Hauptmann, Arthur Schnitzler, and Hugo von Hofmann-stahl. And, in outline and thrust, it projects a general picture of modern drama still acceptable today. Although flawed in particular judgments, the book does not seem outdated as a whole; it is a sturdy pioneer of its subject, a far cry from the backward-looking criticism of his contemporaries, such as Brander Matthews.

His assessment of Strindberg might well be applied to his *Case of Mr. Crump*: "Strindberg's memory clings with a cruel and self-tormenting tenacity to what had given him pain. The result is an observation of life from which we avert our eyes—shamed by its merciless truth" (*Drama*, 27). Strindberg, of course, dealt with the maladies of relationships between men and women.

Though granting the inevitabliity of a Neoromantic and Symbolist revolt against Naturalism, Lewisohn responds especially to the naturalistic trend in modern drama. Ibsen and Strindberg both, he states, reached their peak in naturalistic drama and declined in effectiveness in veering away from it.

Lewisohn's best critical study, in his pre-*Nation* days, was *The Spirit of Modern German Literature* (1916), first delivered as lectures at the University of Wisconsin at the invitation of Professor A. R. Hohlfeld, Chairman of the German Department. One feels it was written *con amore*; the book is rich in content, the product of his many years of reading and teaching German literature. It is, to a large degree, introductory, and devotes space to a summary of novels and other works; indeed, many of the authors taken up are still unknown to the American reading public. But it serves as more than a helpful manual; it also signifies Lewisohn's beginning to turn critically from a flexible and idealistic Naturalism to an emphasis on creative expression, the expressiveness of the individual artist.

Lewisohn begins by asserting that the perennial source of art is the "struggling, agonizing human soul"; literature grows out of "the impassioned experience of life."[9] However, modern German literature began in a quest for doctrinal Naturalism, though Naturalism in Germany had idealistic ends. The early German Naturalists, culminating in Hauptmann, were confirmed meliorists, lacking the pessimism of Naturalists in other countries. After an initial subjection to a doctrinaire Naturalism, German writers affected a "self-contained mastery of their medium"

(*MLG,* 18). They were liberated from Emile Zola into more free forms.

Americans, Lewisohn asserts, can read these works with profit. Neither Upton Sinclair's *The Jungle* nor the American Winston Churchill's *Inside of the Cup,* he claims, compares to *Büttner the Peasant* by Wilhelm von Polenz (1861-1903) or, an even better work, the thesis-novel *Sylvester on Geyer* by Georg von Ompteda (b. 1863). (Ompteda is not listed even now in the *Columbia Dictionary of Modern European Literature.*) Lewisohn discusses as well the anti-Romantic lyric, with an emphasis on Detler Lilliencron (1844-1909) and Otto Julius Bierbaum (1865-1910). He turns his attention again to the dramatists Hauptmann and Schnitzler: "...what other modern dramatists have given as much of the savor of reality, of the living body and soul of man?" (*MGL,* 40). He devotes a chapter to the best three natualistic novelists of Germany to that date: Clara Viebig (b. 1860), the great woman writer of the tradition; Gustav Frenssen (1863-1945), whom Lewisohn designates the ultimate optimist of Naturalism and a prose stylist of a high order; and Thomas Mann, whose first novel, *Buddenbrooks* (1901), tracing the decline of a patrician family of Lübeck merchants, Lewisohn regards as the best German novel in the naturalistic tradition. On Mann, Lewisohn was always prescient; his excellent discussion of *Buddenbrooks* is consistent with his effectiveness generally as an interpreter of Mann.

But, after discussing the Naturalists, Lewisohn turns with special animation to the literature expressive of personality: Richard Dehmel, Rainer M. Rilke, Stefan George, Hugo von Hofmannstahl in poetry, Hesse and Ricarda Huch in fiction. He finally discourses, at some length, on Nietzshe and Goethe, representatives of the tradition of striving (*Streben*) for the higher self. Of Nietzshe, he concludes: "It is clear, then, that even if we strip Nietzsche's work of its questionable metaphysics, and even discount the doctrine of the superman, there is left the noblest and austerest summons to freedom, fortitude and greatness in the personal life that ours, or indeed, any age has known—there is left the inspired philosophic vision of ... free creative personality ... " (*MGL,* 71).

We see, from this quotation, that *The Spirit of Modern German Literature* holds simultaneously the earlier critical credo Lewisohn espoused, that of an expressive Naturalism, with a new emphasis on the creative personality that Lewisohn would stress in his years as an editor for the *Nation.* Goethe, for Lewisohn, mirrors both tendencies at once—an objective rendering of nature and the aspirations for superior accomplishment demonstrated by *Faust.* The spirit of modern German literature, therefore, is twofold: "for in it we find on the one hand, naturalism, cultivation of science, social organization for the collective welfare and practical efficiency ... and on the other hand we find: an individualistic humanism, the cult of beauty ... and a tireless spiritual striving" (*MGL,* 118).

One of the most pleasing of Lewisohn's critical works, *The Spirit of Modern German Literature,* lacks the magisterial authority of the later *Cities and Men* and parts of *Expression in America;* it also, however, to the reader's relief, avoids the combativeness, personal intrusiveness, and Freudian misreadings of some of his later criticism.

French Poets and Continental Critics: Toward Personal Expressiveness

Poets of Modern France (1918), composed while Lewisohn still taught German at Ohio State University, consists of seventy pages of discussion mostly of French Symbolist poets and ninety pages of his original translations of French short poems. It also has, as informative tools, short biographies of the thirty poets translated, a bibliography of secondary sources, mostly French and German, and an index of first lines, both French and English. His aim here, as in his two earlier critical works, is partially pedagogical. His discussion, brief as it is, had few precedents in America, the most notable of which, Amy Lowell's *Six French Poets* (1915), was narrower in scope.

He begins with a new note in his criticism, one that will sound and resound later: "The struggle of man, however blind and stumbling, however checked by tribal rage and tribal terror, is toward self-hood."[10] For the first time an autobiographical impulse asserts itself in the criticism. His unpopular position of neutrality during the War, his subsequent isolation and his need to achieve self-hood, will lead to *Up Stream,* upon which he would soon be at work. In *Poets of Modern France* the chords of resistance and self-assertion are struck. Lewisohn seems to link, in part, his own travails with the *Symbolistes,* who sought a "new freedom and a new music." Citing Remy de Gourmont, he avers that a poet must create his own aesthetic.

His account of the sources of the new poetry follows a standard course, exemplified by the first chapter of Edmund Wilson's *Axel's Castle* (1931): the revolt against the Parnassians, objectivists in poetry, and Naturalism; the influence of Baudelaire's sonnet *Correspondances;* the traces of post-Kantian idealism. Baudelaire's substance had more effect than his form: "His influence upon the future was due to his substance; to the merciless revelation of himself, his stubborn assertion of his strong and morbid soul..." (*Poets,* 12–13). Lewisohn's definition of the *symboliste* is conventional: "the poet is to use the details of the phenomenal world exclusively as symbols of the inner or spiritual reality which it is his aim to project in art" (*Poets,* 9).

Lewisohn's appraisals of various poets, shared by others in his time, would probably bear modifications today. He elevates Paul Verlaine, "the purest lyrical singer that France had ever known," but plays down Stéphane Mallarmé, "a man of a very thin though very fine vein of authentic genius" (*Poets,* 17). He does not mention Paul Valéry, just emerging from a long silence with his *Le Jeune Parque* (1917). Two poets of special merit for Lewisohn are Emile Verhaeren, whom he writes about perceptively, and Henri Régnier. He writes knowledgeably of Moréas, Vielé-Griffin, Merrill, Samain, de Gourmont, Jammes, and Fort.

One feels that, though Lewisohn intends to praise the modern French poets, he withholds a measure of final approval, that he is unwilling to accept *Symbolisme* as a poetry of a major order. Withdrawal—with the exception of Verhaeren—characterizes their work; in exploring the world within, they ignore the world without. For Lewisohn, they are locked, in Wilson's phrase, in Axel's Castle: "... there has been among them no personality so balanced, so fully achieved as to grapple with reality..." (*Poets,* 70). Such a confrontation with reality, he asserts, is the needed next step in French poetry. Lewisohn would desire a poetry "not quite so beautiful but more valorous and severe" (*Poets,* 70).

A Modern Book of Criticism (1919), an anthology of twenty-five French, German, English, and American selections, was the most combative of his critical works to that date. (Lewisohn translated the French and German critics himself, with the exception of a piece by Hofmannsthal.) The Introduction condemns Paul Elmer More and the Humanists, who espoused traditional moral standards in the practice of criticism. Lewisohn eagerly enters into the arena of the Battle of the Books, the ancients versus the moderns, the latter led by Van Wyck Brooks and H. L. Mencken. With a lack neither of vanity nor passion, he declares: "I need no hierarchical moral world for my dwelling place, because I desire neither to judge nor to condemn. Fixed moral standards are useless to him whose central passion is to make men free.... More wants to damn heretics... I do not. His last refuge, like every absolutist at bay, would be in the corporate judgment of mankind. Yes, mankind has let the authoritarians impose on it only too often."[11]

Lewisohn's purpose, in assembling these writings, was to provide ammunition to younger critics against the Humanists, to arm them with "stones for their slings," and also against the Know-nothings, Mencken's "booboisie." (Norman Foerster, a younger disciple of the Humanists, felt, in *Toward Standards,* that Lewisohn was fighting windmills, the dust of battle already settled.) The French critics of Part I—Anatole France, Le Maitre, de Gourmont—make an urbane argument for subjective response on the critic's part; they state the need for personality in criticism. The German critics of Part II—Hebbel, Dilthey, Vol-

kelt, Meyer, Hofmannsthal, Mueller-Freinfels, and Alfred Kerr—
continue the tradition of German Romantic criticism (as well as
English) in stressing the autonomy of the creative imagination.
The English critics of Part III—George Moore (a special admiration of Lewisohn), Bernard Shaw, Arthur Symons, John Galsworthy, Arnold Bennett, W. L. George, MacDonagh, and
Powys—emphasize, on the whole, the need for clarity and realism despite public pressure.

Part IV anthologizes American critics—Huneker, Spingarn,
Mencken, Hackett, Brooks, Bourne, and Lewisohn himself. Char-
acteristically Lewisohn does not try to shade his own light. No
excerpts are selected from the Humanists or critics other than the
"moderns." The Americans Lewisohn draws upon, seemingly the
most embattled of all these critics, declaim against forces that
make American writing difficult: puritanism, the national fear
and dislike of culture, the emphasis on pragmatism.

In one of his *Nation* pieces reprinted here Lewisohn declared
the average American reader to be "an absolutist in morals,
rather tolerant of defections that are not found out, and a prag-
matist in business and politics."[12] Americans, he continues, wrap
themselves in triple-plated armor against spiritual inconven-
ience, and the universities, along with the school of Humanism,
reinforce these tendencies. Lewisohn here reflects his bitter
experience at Columbus, Ohio. In his second selection, "A Note
on Tragedy," he defends modern tragedy on the broadest
grounds. Older tragedy, Greek and Elizabethan, stressed guilt and
punishment, a doctrine acceptable to most Americans; modern
playgoers are less willing to give credence to *Ghosts* or *The
Weavers* or *Justice* because these tragedies are premised on the
fact that tragic figures are victimized by forces beyond their
control. Modern plays evoke feelings of compassion instead of
retribution, and audiences are made less comfortable as a result.
The logic of this argument seems shaky.

Alfred Kazin called *A Modern Book of Criticism* a "valuable
early anthology."[13] Combative in purpose, the set of pieces was
eclectic in kind yet compatible with Lewisohn's critical needs. Of
Lewisohn's position, Charles I. Glicksberg's comment seems

appropriate: "Like Dreiser and Mencken and Van Wyck Brooks, Ludwig Lewisohn warred against puritanism and the tendency of our cultures to stress narrow, parochial, and utilitarian values as opposed to the freedom of the creative life."[14]

Lewisohn versus Amy Lowell

Though Lewisohn proved receptive to innovation and experiment in the drama and in Continental literature, he remained rigidly conservative in appraising new movements in poetry and fiction in English. This anomaly is especially evident in his essay "The Problem of Modern Poetry," which appeared in the *Bookman* in 1919. This essay is followed immediately in the same issue by a countering article by the Imagist poet Amy Lowell, "The Case of Modern Poetry versus Professor Lewisohn." This unusual arrangement was probably sought by the editors. Though Lewisohn's article is elegantly written, Miss Lowell gets the better of argument. Lewisohn was throwing straws against the wind.

Though Lewisohn begins on a note of deceptive sympathy toward the modernists, those in revolt against the Georgian tradition (he names, among others, John Masefield, Robert Frost, Ezra Pound and Miss Lowell), he raises two objections which dominate his presentation. First, he cavils against the tendency of the modernists to fix their attention objectively upon an image or narrative instead of devoting themselves to "impassioned contemplation," which Lewisohn takes to be the true province of poetry. Second, he attacks their desire to resort to an extreme measure to free verse, without falling back upon rhythmic patterns. (He exempts from criticism W.B. Yeats and other Irish poets, who have drawn upon the priceless resource of ancient folk literature.)

He has no antagonism to free verse, he states, but

our contemporary writers of free verse go a step further. They go even beyond the practitioners of impassioned prose. For while the latter employ isochronous rhythm-groups (metrical feet)...our free verse men try not to use such rhythm-groups at all but to make their medium as toneless as possible and to fix attention wholly upon the image and emotion.[15]

Lewisohn asserts his acceptance of free verse, but clearly his personal preferences—to judge by the examples he chooses to praise—are indebted to conventional meters and even rhymes. He praises A.E. Housman, George Meredith, Arthur Symons. One can say that Lewisohn's preferences in peotry did not change after 1919; he has a blind spot in reading twentieth-century poetry in English; also, in reading much of twentieth-century fiction, except for that in the Naturalist tradition.

Amy Lowell correctly perceives that Lewisohn, in trying to present a case against modern poetry, merely expresses a personal preference. His theoretical objections are easily refuted. Narrative is as much the prerogative of poetry as of the short story, and the image or fixed emotion is as much the subject of poetry as impassioned contemplation. In addition, practitioners of modern poetry, including herself, have always insisted upon the place of rhythm in free verse. Lewisohn's initial expression of sympathy is illusory:

One by one he takes up the modern poets, for all the world as though he were handling building stones; he turns them in his hands, exhibits, with a deprecating smile, the inadequacy of each, and lays it down in favor of some other stone, the *débris* of an old and crumbling structure. Picking up these ancient blocks...he slips them into place, and in the end what have we left? A reconstruction of a venerable, classic pile, with all the new, strange stones and their potentialities discarded in the background.[16]

If Lewisohn had been always so hostile to innovation, he would have left no mark as a critic.

Drama and the Stage: The Drama Critic at Work

In 1919 Villard invited Lewisohn to become theater critic of the *Nation*; probably his most telling recommendation for the post was his *Modern Drama* (1915). Carl Van Doren, literary editor for the same journal, wrote of Lewisohn as critic as follows: "Night after night he went patiently to the theater, enduring bad and mediocre entertainments for the sake of an occasional play worth writing about in his weekly notice. Almost every week he wrote a review of a book, generally a novel. He was no less a journalist for being a scholar and an artist.... But Lewisohn was alert as a hawk, seeing better because he lived naturally in the upper air. He touched nothing that he did not elevate...."[17] Joseph Wood Krutch, in appraising the work, called Lewisohn "the most significant of our dramatic critics."[18] Barrett H. Clark, in *European Theories of the Drama* (1947), wrote: "Lewisohn's familiarity with European literature and philosophy enabled him to apply standards to the American drama of which few 'regular' dramatic critics were aware."[19]

It was Lewisohn's misfortune to assume the desk of drama critic when America had no outstanding playwrights. Eugene O'Neill was just beginning to make an impact, and Lewisohn lauded *Beyond The Horizon*. In light of the revolutionary theater in Europe, the contrast was painful. The American stage was given over to farce, melodrama, and arresting sets, intended to stir immediate pleasure without thought.

Drama and the Stage (1922), a collection of his pieces from the *Nation*, provides models of good drama criticism. Lewisohn points up judiciously the failings of the American theater at that time, encourages promising playwrights, and reviews specific plays thoroughly, summarizing the events of each play and the acting in terms of a well-defined critical idea.

Mechanics, he writes, dominate the American theater: "Revolving stages, subtle lights, elaborate scenes are in their right order beautiful and useful things. They become a menace when they cause it to be forgotten that the platform is the platform of the eternal poet struggling with the mysteries of earth. This is not fine language; it is the plain and sober truth. But who will admit it?"[20] Apparently, not George Jean Nathan, who seeks "a 'gentleman's paradise' of intelligent entertainment, but without philosophical ideas." Not Brander Matthews, who applies rigidly "certain historical analogies," and never Percy Hammond.

David Belasco, the perfect mechanic of the theater, pays strict attention to lighting and production, but has not produced one work of a great dramatist. The same can be said for the more pretentious Gordon Craig. The dean of American playwrights, August Thomas, follows the formulae of the well-made play in the worst tradition of the French theater. Dialogue in the theater is second-rate. The average American playwright uses "semi-naturalistic dialogue romanticized by a bad tradition drawn from both plays and books" (DS, 37).

Too many actors seek merely to display their personalities; they all want to be John Barrymores. An interesting section examines revivals of Shakespeare. Lewisohn admires E. H. Sothern's Hamlet, "a stricken idealist...a pure soul whose moral world has been riven beyond mending" (DS, 127-28). He is less taken with John Barrymore's Richard III. Barrymore dazzles, but misses a note of ultimate sincerity. Although Barrymore is a great reader of verse, his acting suffers "from a display of personal idiosyncracy and untempered power" (DS, 136). Lionel Barrymore (whom Lewisohn otherwise admired) interprets Macbeth in a manner "rough, sordid, unintelligent, ignoble. He is not a hero caught in the coils of fate; he is a beast in a trap" (DS, 138).

In a digression, Lewisohn writes of the moviemaker, D. W. Griffith, whom he finds a representative American. Griffith projects the "moral littleness and the physical magnificence, the intellectual sloth and the mechanical speed" (DS, 111) characteristic of the American personality.

Of contemporary American playwrights, Lewisohn pays particular attention to Susan Glaspell. Her early plays, he states, are strong but meager in expression. Her later play, Inheritors, is an important study of a significant American issue—the tragic disintegration of New England idealism over three generations. Clarence Dane's Bill of Divorcement (1921) is good but loses tragic character because of accidental interpositions. Arthur

Richman's *Ambush* (1921) is a memorable play subjected to unsympathetic reviews.

Lewisohn reserves his greatest praise for successful revivals of the "Lonely Classics" and modern Continental plays. His essay on the *Medea* of Euripides is excellent though somewhat subjective, siding with Jason who will not acknowledge his weariness with an overbearing wife. He deplores the neglect of Gay's witty *Beggar's Opera*. He renders sound analyses of Shaw's *Heartbreak House* and *Back to Methuselah* and records the decline of James Barrie to the level of popular entertainer. His chronicle of the German stage from 1911 to 1919 is sympathetic, with words of commendation for Wedekind, Kaiser, and Expressionism. He is moved by the Theater Guild productions of Strindberg's *Dance of Death*, though he feels that the actors do not always understand their parts, and of Ferenc Molnár's *Liliom*, and of Arthur Hopkins's production of Gorki's *Night Lodging*, with the probing art of the actors Alan Dinehart, Pauline Lord, and Edward G. Robinson.

Drama and the Stage reveals Lewisohn's criticism near his best: his "lucidity of mind," his elevated standards, his meticulous analysis of particular plays, books, and traditions. It is the best examination extant of the American theater in the immediate postwar period.

Some *Nation* Pieces

If the reader turns to the *Nation* magazine for material not included in *The Drama and the Stage*, some miscellaneous pieces are worthy of note.

Lewisohn saw approximately one hundred plays a season. The most striking of American playwrights for him was Eugene O'Neill, at the beginning of his career, whom Lewisohn dubbed the first true Naturalist of the American stage; one of his last reviews was of *All God's Chillun*, confirming the promise of *Beyond the Horizon*. Lewisohn thought well, too, of Zona Gale's *Miss Lulu Bett*. Though especially attuned to Naturalism he applauds the Expressionism of Elmer Rice's *The Adding Machine*, defining the term.

The breadth of his interest and knowledge of foreign drama is striking, evidenced by excellent reviews of Tolstoi's *Power of Darkness* and Ferenc Molnár's *Liliom*. He has high praise for the Jewish Art Theater, its plays given in Yiddish, free from the commercialism of the Broadway stage. This last interest undoubtedly led to his translation of David Pinski's *The Treasure*. To testify to Broadway's commercialism, a representative Lewisohn article is "The Cult of Prettiness," discussing the desire of producers to put on pretty plays for pretty performers like Billie Burke and Laurette Taylor.

In miscellaneous articles and reviews he maintained his interest in German literature, including Goethe and Heine, and French poetry. On the other hand, as a noteworthy phenomenon, his reviews of American fiction show a much more parochial attitude. He reviewed mostly novels such as he himself would write: realistic and conventional, concentrating on problems of love and marriage. He praises Henry G. Ackman's *Zell* (1921), Floyd Dell's *Janet March* (1924), Frank Swinnerton's *Coquette* (1924), Edgar Lee Masters's *Mirage* (1924), Sherwood Anderson's *Horses and Men* (1924)—the last the only distinctive fiction in the lot. The contrast between the cosmopolitan critic and the parochial novelist seeking models and counterparts is illuminating. Interestingly, he rejects Evelyn Scott's *Narcissus* (1922) because it attempts to probe the unconscious; the rationalist side of man, he writes, is the novelist's true concern. Evidently, he was not to fall disciple to Freud until later, while sojourning in Europe.

In a review of *Mein Weg als Deutscher und Yude* by Jacob Wasserman, Lewisohn (July 21, 1921), deploring Wasserman's lack of concern for Judaism, advocates the pluralist argument soon to appear in *Up Stream*. The Jew should not try to identify with the majority; such an attempt weakens the cause of all minorities. The Jew, granted his own point of view, should try to cooperate with all groups. But —as stated in a later article, "A Jew Meditates" (February 20, 1924)—neither Jew nor Gentile can be saved by "rituals of metaphysical assumptions." The Jew must embrace peace, internationalism, and humanism. This article, as late as 1924, precedes and differs considerably from *Israel* (1925), in which Lewisohn embraces Zionism and appreciates the religious fervor of Polish Jews. Again, evidence is presented that Lewisohn's travels in Europe in late 1924 and 1925 turned him into a more ardent advocate of Judaism.

An essay on South Carolina (July 12, 1922) casts a nostalgic look at Charleston as it used to be; the new South is more vulgar and ugly. "A race lived here that loved dignity ... books and wine and human distinction. Its sins, which were many, fade into the past."

A review of Benedetto Croce's *Ariosto, Shakespeare, and Corneille* (June 18, 1921) rejects Croce's idealistic aesthetics as too disembodied, ignoring the artist's will in favor only of the aesthetic idea. Lewisohn's *The Creative Life* will espouse an art of autobiographical origins, revealing the interaction of artist and society.

Lewisohn's articles for the *Nation*, aside from his dramatic criticism, reflect his ongoing concerns.

The Creative Life: A Theory of Literature

The Creative Life (1924), dedicated to Thelma Spear, chiefly derives from columns written for magazines; Chapter 1 and the first section of Chapter 4 first appeared in the Literary Review of the *New York Evening Post*. The book puts forth a theory of literature, as against the practical criticism evidenced in Lewisohn's earlier work. Lewisohn here does not vary radically from the premises underlying *The Spirit of Modern German Literature*, but his emphasis falls more on the creative sources of art rather than on the mimetic approach implicit in a doctrine of Naturalism.

In his prologue he declares himself a radical in life, a classicist in literature. A "radical" as he employs the term would more properly be defined as a "liberal" today; a "radical" in his use wishes to do away with "hoary prejudices" and to remediate "moral suffering." A "classicist" might be more accurately defined as a "conservative," and Lewisohn seizes the chance to state that he finds Joyce and Woolf unintelligible; he also cannot understand the viewpoint of such "mystics" as Jacob Wasserman (whom he translated). Strangely, Lewisohn, so responsive to experiment in French and German and in European drama, was unsympathetic to literary innovations in English. He particularly disliked D. H. Lawrence, who was achieving more successfully in some of his novels what Lewisohn was trying to do; even Amy Lowell and the Imagists he found too unconventional for his taste.

In any event, literature, no matter how personal to the artist, has to have an ultimate social purpose: "... as time goes on, I care less and less for art in its most abstract forms and more and more for life. I am too preoccupied to be held by anything that approaches the decorative."[21]

Clearly, Lewisohn's approach to art is experiential, i.e., the writer derives his subject matter from his own experiences or autobiography. The creative mind builds on experience and "gives the vision of that experience to mankind." Interpreting experience in a fresh or original way must bring the artist into opposition with the solid citizenry, who have compartmentalized experience to avoid surprise.

Contradictions appear between Lewisohn's theoretical statements and his expressions of literary preference. Although he states that artists are all romantics at heart, for "the Universe, as William James finely said, is as wild as a hawk's wing," his personal predilection in English literature is the eighteenth century; the work of criticism he especially admires is Samuel Johnson's *Lives of the Poets*. Although he advocates experiment in fiction ("Liberation can obey no law but an inherent one ..."), he feels most at home with the realistic, even plum pudding, novel: Butler's *Way of All Flesh*, Maugham's *Of Human Bondage*, Galsworthy's *Forsythe Saga*. Among American writers he praises Edith Wharton, Sinclair Lewis, and Theodore Dreiser. A romantic idealist in theory, he is a realist by inclination. As said before, he is more pliant in judging Continental literature. Much of the book is devoted to an attack on "ancestral pieties," a view characteristic of the 1920s and ironic in light of his later conversion to traditional Judaism.

The essential inconsistency of the work—his defense of the creative mind together with his lack of sensitivity to many of the creative currents in the period—mar the work and make it less useful than *Drama and the Stage* and *The Spirit of Modern German Literature.* One passage from *The Creative Life* about American literature, concerned with Emerson, Thoreau, and Whitman, he would have done well to keep in mind when writing *Expression in America.* He speaks of a need to reevaluate American literature and recognize its progressive promises: "We have a national past to cultivate, a past dedicated to freedom, to the right of revolution, to the creative life in its widest and fullest sense."[22]

Cities and Men: Toward Humanism

Cities and Men (1927) is possibly the best of Lewisohn's critical books, with effective travel sketches of European cities and mature literary studies of writers to whom he responded most in his literary career. If the reader were asked to recommend one of Lewisohn's books of criticism above the rest, this is the book he might select.

The first chapter, "Culture and Barbarism: An Irrelevant Introduction," attempts to reconcile the disparities of *The Creative Life.* Whether the attempt grew from further introspection or from the suggestion of others, one cannot ascertain. Lewisohn was sensitive to what he believed was informed criticism from those around him.

Here again he defends "subjective" literature against so-called "objective" standards. "Why do the critics distrust the modern autobiographical instinct...?" Lewisohn cites writers, such as Tolstoy, whose works were "one long confession." Of course, though art derives from life, art diverges from life because of its form and interpretive qualities. "When the work is finished...it has become transposed into another and more intelligible world; it has become detached from the world of mere reality...."[23] He goes further, moreover, by embracing Mann and Dreiser as "subjective" writers. Even Samuel Johnson speaks in the "eternal individual human voice." Autobiography is not inconsistent with realism and Naturalism, for realism and Naturalism find their source in personal pain. Thus Lewisohn strives to unify the sometimes inconsistent strands of expressiveness and Naturalism in his outlook.

The real barbarism in literature is the pseudoclassical which disguises past paganism and historical cruelties as forms of tradition and order. *Cities and Men*, written in Europe, records Lewisohn's discovery of aspects of historical experience even more disturbing than the provincial rigidities of American life. He saw beautiful, now decadent, cities that glorified past wars and organized peacetime savagery. The art that glorifies a wicked past, he concluded, is a bad art; only the voice of reason and humanity deserves to be heeded. "Men read epic and ballad and classical tragedy or see cathedrals of the Middle Ages and admire ferocity in war and the obedience of henchmen and uninquiring faith in baseless myth. They read Amos and Socrates, Montaigne and Goethe and Whitman, and they are set free for the pursuit of goodness and truth" (*CM*, 13).

Looking back to Matthew Arnold, Lewisohn sees the ultimate distinction between good and bad art as that between an art that promotes culture and an art that sustains barbarism. During his years on the *Nation* an opponent of Humanism, Lewisohn is now shaping a humanism of his own. It it needless to harp on inconsistencies. As is well-known, even critics of the highest order—a Plato, a Wordsworth, a Coleridge—are sometimes inconsistent and also subject to change. Critics of a lesser order, like Lewisohn, are even more rarely of one piece. Lewisohn began as an exponent of a nondoctrinaire naturalism, which never lost its attraction for him, then advocated an art of personal experience, and then propounded a new humanism. Strangely, while beginning his first chapter with a defense of expressiveness which embraces realism and Naturalism as well, at the end of the chapter he almost abandons the autonomy of art altogether, subordinating art to the realm of reason, humanity, and wholeness of personality.

In one of his travel sketches, viewing Venice recalls to him Shelley's definition of history, "that record of crimes and tyrannies." He comments: "Could Italy or the world once more be freed from the oppressor, could one lasting blow for liberty and peace and mercy be struck at such a price, I would stand unmoved while this golden beauty, which stirs and haunts my soul no less than others', toppled forever into the overwhelming sea" (*CM*, 273). But, the reader might respond, the choice is purely hypothetical; no one demands a choice between Venice and a more rational world order. Police states are indifferent to Venice's existence and would not offer to abandon their prerogatives if Venice disappears.

Lewisohn expresses this idea in more moving fashion when writing of Georg Brandes: "He knows with Anatole France that history and criticism, like poetry and music, are but part of that visionary pageantry by which man makes human... the naked and inhuman world" (*CM*, 196). For Lewisohn Europe presented a spectacle of beauty mixed with terror. Even Vienna, which he loved, "has those old unhappy far-off things in common with all the wretched and tragic cities of men." Europe taught lessons in man's inhumanity to man and in the nakedness of man without faith well beyond his American experience.

Cities and Men: Literary Sketches

The literary sketches of *Cities and Men* are assembled from a miscellany of writers Lewisohn had learned to appreciate in a lifetime of reading. Beginning with English authors, he first writes most illuminatingly of William Hazlitt. The occasion of his essay was the publication of P. P. Howe's biography of Hazlitt (1922).

With a spirit of identification derived from events in his own life, Lewisohn defends *Liber Amoris*, Hazlitt's account of his infatuation with a servant girl which traditionally embarrassed even Hazlitt's admirers. Hazlitt's reputation has suffered, Lewisohn claims, because of the "dim presence of old misunderstandings and forgotten slanders." He continues: "His matchless sagacity about men and affairs, his racy eloquence unborrowed but of the ardor of his mind and his heart, his consummate services to creative criticism—these things almost persuaded Stevenson to undertake a biography. But Stevenson's squeamishness was offended by the *Liber Amoris*" (*CM*, 21-22).

Lewisohn proceeds to explain psychologically Hazlitt's relations with women. Shy with women and possessed of a low self-esteem in their company, Hazlitt pursued girls of the lower classes. He married Miss Sarah Stoddard at her initiative, and the marriage proved a dismal failure. (The analogy to Lewisohn's life is obvious.) In 1822, at the age of 44, Hazlitt fell in love with Sarah Walker of *Liber Amoris* fame, and got a divorce, only to discover that Miss Walker had welcomed another lover during their relationship. Lewisohn writes: "The situation may have its aspect of humor from without; it is pure tragedy from within" (*CM*, 27).

Hazlitt's enemies also resented his political ideas, especially his pro-pacifist position during the Napoleonic Wars. Imagine Hazlitt's stance, Lewisohn advises, as a "publicist and critic in 1917, and Hazlitt's case is clear enough." Again, Lewisohn seems to identify his own case with Hazlitt's. He applauds Hazlitt's political integrity, his unswerving regard for truth and liberty whatever political currents prevailed. Hazlitt's political ideas and marital complications have affected men's perception of his critical genius and talents as a man of letters. Drawing insight from his own experience, Lewisohn's essay is an excellent treatment of Hazlitt's critical reputation, but unfortunately has been disregarded or forgotten.

Lewisohn's essay on Matthew Arnold, though good, is less notable, for it breaks no new ground. Arnold's influence, he writes, has been thoroughly absorbed; he discovered the eternal Philistine. "He discovered Main Street; he discovered Babbitt; he discovered Mr. Mencken's neo-Puritanism, reformers, hundred-per-centers." Lewisohn sympathizes, as one might expect, with Arnold's suffering the belittlement of critics like Frederic Harrison, who encapsulated Arnold as an "elegant Jeremiah." The essay admires Arnold's poems, which sensitively record the poet's loss of religious faith. Lewisohn writes: "Granting that the son of Arnold of Rugby was more troubled over the decay of Christian dogma than we are, it should be remembered that that decay symbolized for him a fact of equal gravity to ourselves—the loss of a rational universe in which to be at home" (*CM*, 36).

Also in Lewisohn's pantheon stands John Morley, the last of the English Rationalists, who opposed the First World War. Lewisohn, too, does honor to George Saintsbury, who, although a Tory and not a prose stylist, was sound in literary matters and receptive to all good literature. In contrast to Saintsbury, Lewisohn points to Edmund Gosse, who tried to impose unswerving standards upon literature.

Lewisohn then turns to American writers. He attacks George Santayana, who, in his *Little Essays*, edited by Logan Pearsall Smith in collaboration with the author, seems impervious to American and Germanic cultures. He finds in Santayana's blending of paganism and romanticized Latin culture a "consummate gesture and a triumph of ordered speech," but unsuited to modern needs. Similarly, he sees Jean Cocteau's return to a romanticized Catholicism a retreat from the present. On Santayana and Cocteau, Lewisohn is led on by basic antipathies.

His essay in this section called "American Memories" is richer in value. He draws a picture of the Southern literary climate when he was growing up: the division "between literature and life was...complete. And what was true of South Carolina was true of the country at large." Of course, Lewisohn reverses his juvenile treatment of Southern literature published in a Charleston journal many years before. His memoir of Dreiser, also in this section, has documentary significance and was reprinted in Alfred Kazin's and Charles Shapiro's collection *The Stature of Theodore Dreiser* (1955). The Dreiser Lewisohn knew in the 1910s was a man of great compassion, with a "vast, brooding, sorrowful...vision of life." What Dreiser lacked in formal style he compensated for in universal passion and largeness of heart. Dreiser had asked Lewisohn to write a study of him, but publishers were cold to the idea. That Lewisohn never wrote such a full-length study is a loss, for the Lewisohn of the twenties would have proved an ideal reader of the novelist.

In Europe Lewisohn displayed, in the essay "American in Europe," a yearning for American scenes and literature. In contrast to American literature, he writes, Europeans have turned away from healthy currents; their literature was sodden with "romanticism, with a false and violent historical-mindedness, infected by the political extremes of right and left." As noted before, Lewisohn's exile in Europe was not happy.

Part III, *Germans*, is unusually well informed, with a stress on German liberals not yet poisoned by more recent currents. He writes with affection of the poet Richard Dehmel, of Hauptmann, and particularly of Thomas Mann. His piece on Mann, wrote the reviewer Robert Morse Lovett, himself a critic of Mann (*Bookman*, June 1929), was "written long before the German novelist had received adequate attention in America." Lewisohn writes of the antitheses in Mann's fiction; his was an early expression of a now well-established perception of Mann's fiction: "It is the mind of a lyrical nature constantly transcending itself by sheer force of intellect and artistic self-discipline. It is a nature that yearns for music. But another strain in that nature fears music as a weakness, as mere emotionalism, as self-abandonment" (*CM*, 133). With the *Magic Mountain* Mann turns to human society itself and, with a "vigilant nobility of spirit," focuses on the increasingly disastrous spectacle of modern Europe—a view Lewisohn shared or learned from. In an essay on "Death in Venice," not included here but written as an introduction to that work for its American publication, Lewisohn wrote that Mann had achieved the "miracle of art, which life must imitate if our civilization is to be saved."[24]

In Rilke, whom Lewisohn was one of the first to appreciate in the English-speaking world, Lewisohn found a religious view that moved him deeply: "This strictly modern mystic wants no abrogation of the natural order. The natural order is the divine order" (*CM*, 149). This oneness of man, nature, and God Lewisohn also recognized in Martin Buber, the German Jewish theologian who was to exert a profound influence upon him.

In Part IV: *Frenchmen* Lewisohn adds little to our knowledge of Flaubert, whose concern for style Lewisohn saw as essentially a quest for controlling reality. On Baudelaire, Lewisohn concentrates on Baudelaire's record of torment stirred by guilt and a sense of sin; thus, Lewisohn anticipates T. S. Eliot's "Baudelaire" (1932), with the difference that Eliot saw Baudelaire's torment as the first step in a religious search while Lewisohn saw it as an unhealthy inhibition. "His soul wandered in a thick throttling mist" (*CM*, 173).

Part V: *Jews* is more rewarding than the preceding section. His essay on Heine is fine, a study of a shattering division of soul. Heine was not angelic; the man and the work were the same— "full of pain, warped by wrong, the reverse of Olympian... but also possessing a somber glow, less beautiful than portentous..." (*CM*, 193). Georg Brandes was the good European as critic, who saw the history of mankind embodied in its literature, but refused to adopt a single theory, "like Taine or Villemain or Sherer..." (*CM*, 195).

Lewisohn's last essay is on Martin Buber, who was to have a general philosophical impact a generation later. Lewisohn admires Buber's search for unity, a "Secret Judaism," which flowed forth in the patriarchs, the prophets, the Essenes, the founders of Hassidism. Judaism, to Buber, is not simply imposed externally, but is an inner response of the spirit to the divine order. Undoubtedly, Buber had much to do with Lewisohn's own return to Judaism.

Many of the literary sketches ring with authority, and several—on Mann, Heine, Buber—perhaps deserve the appellation "classic." They are eclectic in attitude, reflecting the many sides of Lewisohn's interests—ranging from an appreciation of Morley's liberal rationalism to Buber's religious mysticism. They reflect Lewisohn's distress at the growing irrationality of contemporary Europe and, in the essays on Rilke and Buber, his growing religiosity. One might say that Lewisohn tries to align the best traditions of the past—both rational and religious—to combat the false gods, Fascism, Communism, and nihilism, of the present.

Conclusion

In the critical works of his academic career, especially at Ohio State University, Lewisohn propounded a theory of nondoctrinaire naturalism, especially discernible in modern German literature, which served as an antidote to the genteel and sentimental tradition in American literature. In his *Nation* years (1919-1924) Lewisohn militantly joined forces with the moderns against the Humanists, who, to Lewisohn's thinking, tried to constrict creativity by imposing fixed standards. In *Cities and Men*, the best critical work of his European exile, Lewisohn, distressed by the contemporary spectacle abroad, became a kind of humanist himself and revealed a growing religiosity. It was in Europe that Lewisohn returned to Judaism. His critical career was not so simple nor diagrammatic as these few sentences might suggest. Earlier attitudes extend themselves into the later work, and sometimes later attitudes can be extrapolated from earlier work. Lewisohn himself deplored a critic with a single theory.

Chapter Five
Lewisohn as Critic II: Toward Symbol and Myth

Lewisohn's major critical work of the 1930s was *Expression in America* (1932), a literary history of the United States that employed eclectically critical approaches derived from the anti-Puritan rebellion of the early twenties, the Naturalism of Dreiser and the Europeans, the discoveries of Freud, and the Humanism evident in *Cities and Men*. Lewisohn seemed to assemble all his critical resources, past and present, to undertake his most ambitious critical enterprise.

Subsequent to *Expression in America*, upon which he had been working intermittently for some five years, Lewisohn turned increasingly as critic to a stress on symbol and myth; he paid tribute to Otto Rank, the psychoanalyst, for leading him in this direction, though most readers have followed the same route through the works of Ernst Cassirer, Suzanne Langer, and Northrop Frye. Lewisohn's work most concerned with "word" and "myth" was the late *The Magic Word* (1950). Clearly, Lewisohn did not remain steadfast with one critical theory for thirty years, but responded, in his own fashion—often reinforced by his evolving attitudes and needs outside of criticism—to the shifting cultural trends of succeeding decades.

Expression in America: The Would-be Masterwork

Expression in America, Lewisohn's personal history of American literature, appeared in 1932; in 1939, for the Modern Library edition, he included a new, long, last chapter bringing the volume to the present and changed the title to *The Story of American Literature*. In the preface he stated that his interest in American literature had taken hold when he was a member of a seminar conducted by Professor Trent at Columbia University; the plan for the book took shape in 1927. He thought of this long study, over 600 pages in length, as the culmination of his critical endeavors.

Undoubtedly, the book has merit, written at the height of Lewisohn's confidence in his critical abilities. Precise and lucid in style, it is eminently readable, still retaining the arresting quality Franklin P. Adams saluted in his Conning Tower column in the New York *Herald Tribune* (March 19, 1932):

"So at the office until 3, and so home and read L. Lewisohn's 'Expression in America,' which I thought the best and most interesting book of American writers I had ever read. And though I think he had prejudices and predilections that color his view of many writers, I doubt that criticism of any other sort is worth a whoop . . . and I think the one thing he lacks is a sense of merriment. . . ."

The last sentence echoes the usual truism. One does not look to F.P.A. for authoritative criticism, but he correctly suggests that Lewisohn relies more on original judgment than on historical or literary scholarship. This independence is sometimes rewarding, linked with the author's obvious love of literature, his extensive curiosity, and his wide range of cultural reference. But the work falls in esteem when one compares it, for example, with D.H. Lawrence's *Studies in Classic American Literature* (1923), another original approach to American writing. Lewisohn lacked Lawrence's gifted set of values on love and life generally and Lawrence's sense of the mythic relevance of American classics.

Critical ingenuity or originality must be based ultimately on a philosophical core; in contrast to Lawrence's rich store of values, Lewisohn applied an eclectic group of criteria consisting of a primitive Freudianism, Arnold's notion that literature serves as a surrogate for moral or scriptural traditions, and a liberal rationalism and progressivism opposed to aristocratic or reactionary tendencies. Many of his judgments derive from the now outworn prejudices of his day, the anti-puritanical sentiments of his contemporaries and their aversion to American literature before

Whitman. The final result mixes invigorating statements with eccentricities. To one commencing a study of American litera- ture, *Expression in America* is unreliable; the professional scholar must carefully sift the good from the bad. It is lively and sometimes exceptional, but also at times marred or outdated.

It is often classified as an illustration of Freudian criticism; certainly Lewisohn states his Freudian views openly in his pref- ace: "It was equally inevitable that I use the organon or method of knowledge associated with the venerated name of Sigmund Freud."[1] Several of his definitions of literature suggest Freudian derivation: literature as a personal expression originating in a neurosis or compensating for it. Many of his most flagrant judgments are Freudian. His forerunners in this school of criti- cism were F. D. Prescott's *The Poetic Mind* (1920), Van Wyck Brooks's *The Ordeal of Mark Twain* (1920), and J. W. Krutch's *Edgar Allan Poe* (1926). Louis Fraiberg, in *Psychoanalysis and American Literary Criticism*, thinks these early psychological critics approached their subjects too naively.[2]

But Lewisohn's preface also incorporates the views of the later Matthew Arnold, as exemplified in "The Study of Poetry" (1880). Literature, in Arnold's elevated view, provides a substitute for religious codes now in decline. Lewisohn writes: "... literature was no longer an elegant diversion or an illustration of the foreknown or fixed but moral research, a road to salvation, the bread of life" (*SAL*, ix). The last part of the work, especially, including the long last chapter inveighing against the chaos of modern literature, owes more to Arnold than to Freud. Lewi- sohn's growing emphasis on spiritual values in literature might account as well for his later change of title, dropping the more Freudian *Expression in America* for the more neutral *Story of American Literature*.

Lewisohn's work does not have the historical perspective of V. L. Parrington's *Main Currents of American Thought* (3 vols., 1927-1930); indeed, the study has been criticized for the degree with which it ignores historical backgrounds; but it does have a liberal and progressive stance not usually noticed. Thus, in his preface, he attacks Edith Wharton—though long an admiration of his—as a snob (a judgment later corrected by Edmund Wilson) and praises, further on in the book, Emerson and Thoreau for their attack on social and economic conventions. On social and political grounds, Parrington and he are compatible.

Ultimately, Lewisohn judges each author's work in terms of a flexible definition of the term *classic*. To summarize for him, a classic is perennially humane, both intellectually and emotionally rewarding, and as finished in form as it is satisfying in content. With such a standard, Lewisohn found Thomas Mann a "classic." But even praiseworthy authors might fall short because of certain deficiencies: Whitman, for eccentricity of form; Twain, for intellectual inadequacies in his later work; Hanry James, for emotional lacks; Edith Wharton, for social biases. To be a classic, one must escape the Freudian pitfall, that is, he must not be dominated by neurosis; he must meet Arnold's requirement that the artist project an enhancing idea; and he must meet the Romantic requirement of personal expression objectified by symbol and form. Holding to so demanding a set of criteria, Lewisohn contradicts what he had fought for strongly in the past, as in *A Modern Book of Criticism*: the artist's right to develop in his own way. Apparently, Lewisohn abandons impressionistic grounds of criticism.

Lewisohn's initial discussion, of the Puritan writers of New England, is an extended harangue. The Puritans, who came to America bearing with them a narrowed Protestant culture of the post-Renaissance period, were repressive, "bearing down with unparalleled harshness upon the more amiable and expansive forces of human nature" (*SAL*, xxxi). Puritanism contradicted literature, for literature depends on humane outlooks which the movement did not recognize. Lewisohn has little to say of Anne Bradstreet and understandably was unaware of Edward Taylor, the best of early New England poets. As disturbing as Lewisohn's sweeping condemnation of Puritanism is his tying it to many modern phenomena he disapproves of: "the labor spy, the liquor spy, the Ku Klux Klan guardian and whipper of his fellows" (*SAL*, 2). Puritanism, for the author, embraces everything negative in American life: "Always, from the witchhunts in seventeentth-century Massachusetts to recent whippings and shootings of the Ku Klux Klan, these outbursts have been characterized by a hectic torment, a sexual symbolism and an ambivalence that stamps them with the unmistakable stamp of the Puritan conflict" (*SAL*, 15). To be sure, Lewisohn was not alone in this denunciation of Puritanism; Mencken, Ernest Boyd, and almost a generation of critics assisted him. Lewisohn carried this attitude over from the early 1920s.

On the other hand, Lewisohn praises the early settlers of Pennsylvania: William Penn, Pastorius, and the German pietists. "The German settlers were Christians and had music in their souls" (*SAL*, 23). Professor Oscar Cargill felt that Lewisohn's acknowledgment of the Pennsylvania settlers was a welcome contribution. Lewisohn also commends Benjamin Franklin, who had a "strong and acute instinct for literary form." Though the critic has reservations about Franklin's utilitarianism, he sees him, especially in his later years, as "the first civilized American." Lewisohn's discussion of Franklin is more encompassing than D. H. Lawrence's.

Lewisohn thought that the period of the Revolution left no significant creative record. With anti-Federalist feeling, he assessed the Federalist Papers as having merely historical value. "Alexander Hamilton and his associates were not only Calvinists, but aristocrats." Like Charles Beard, Lewisohn opposed those who upheld the concept of property as primary. His sympathies leaned toward the Democrats. Paine was "extraordinarily readable" and useful; his deism, "unlovely" but superior to the "superstitions" he was attacking. An even greater figure was the philosophical libertarian, Thomas Jefferson. Another democratic spirit, Crévecoeur, maintained a view of American life more idyllic than realistic; he expressed the perennial hope of immigrants coming to America, "which our generation has done its best forever to destroy"—a reference to the restrictive immigration acts of 1924. Philip Freneau, though a liberal, was basically mediocre. Lewisohn's attitudes toward the colonial period were traditionally liberal, somewhat one-sided, sharing the defects of the liberal imagination Lionel Trilling sought later to redress.

He held the romancers Fenimore Cooper and William Gilmore and Simms in low esteem: "...invention in regard to pursuit and capture and physical combat are all that Cooper has to offer. Natty Bumppo is a less than human characterization" (*SAL*, 55-56). Here, again, Lawrence reveals what Lewisohn missed: Cooper's myth-making quality. Lewisohn also sacrificed Washington Irving, representing the gentry and offering escape from reality; Irving leads Lewisohn to the genteel tradition, infected with Puritanism. The critic thought of Bryant more favorably because of Bryant's "liberality in thought."

Book II, "The Polite Writers," pools together miscellaneous writers from Irving and Longfellow to Brander Matthews and Woodrow Wilson; these lack "all contact with reality" and feebly consent "to a world of chaos and distraction." The polite writers include Oliver Wendell Holmes, James Russell Lowell, Henry Timrod, Sidney Lanier, Richard Watson Gilder; an exception is made of John Greenleaf Whittier because of his staunch liberal convictions. Oscar Cargill has rightly objected to this procrustean measuring of different writers from different periods. To these writers Lewisohn brings more invective than analysis. In contrast, he praises the autobiography of P. T. Barnum, frontier literature, and Negro spirituals for their closeness to life and freedom from gentility.

Book III, "The Transcendental Revolt: Emerson and Thoreau," bears Lewisohn's first extended analysis. Both writers are "classics," though with extensive shortcomings. Lewisohn dislikes transcendentalism, which he views as an extension of Puritanism, though with a lesser emphasis on guilt, and believes the chapter on "Higher Laws" ruins Thoreau's otherwise great book, *Walden*. Both New Englanders were defective as men, "chilled under-sexed valetudinarians." Emerson lacked "intensity," an absorption in the "concrete coil of things." Thoreau was "intellectually one of the bravest men that ever lived, and also a clammy prig." (*SAL*. 136). Lewisohn thought best of Emerson and Thoreau as social critics and rebels, the authors of "Self-Reliance" and "Civil Disobedience." He admires their liberal strain, but otherwise seems to measure them by the standards of early twentieth-century Naturalism.

Though many remember solely his depictions of Emerson and Thoreau as "under-sexed valetudinarians," one should not ignore the many insights Lewisohn brings to these authors. "Self-Reliance," which he calls "the most revolutionary document in modern literature," began a central tradition in American letters. He speaks of Emerson's farsightedness, his seer-like ability to comprehend almost everything, including his own shortcomings. If he dislikes Emerson's metaphysical idealism, he enjoys his wit. He praises *English Traits*. Of Emerson on poetry, he writes: "Emerson set forth the still neglected but inevitable notion of literature as a continuous interpretation of experience in a dynamic world" (*SAL*, 129). He speaks of Emerson's small body of verse as "not yet perhaps quite equaled by any formal poet in America." His remarks on individual poems are penetrating.

Thoreau, to Lewisohn, is a great prose stylist who embodies the best tradition of individualism and freedom from materialism, but who lacks passion. "His simplicity and courage have a faint icy pathos." From a modern perspective, one can disagree with Lewisohn. The Thoreau of *Walden* and "Civil Disobedience" rings with a passionate conviction; there are other passions than the sexual. On Emerson and Thoreau, Lewisohn's Freudian bell-ringing detracts from an otherwise good discussion.

Book IV, "The Troubled Romancers," concerned with Edgar Allan Poe, Nathaniel Hawthorne, and Herman Melville, is the section in *Expression in America* that readers today would find most alien. All three are classified as neurotics who chose flight and fantasy to escape real-life problems: "Was it the quality of American life or was it wholly their own natures which drove these three into expression that has structure of a neurosis?" They were not "human enough" and were "romancers because they were hopelessly imprisoned in their unconscious conflicts" (*SAL*, 154-55).

Lewisohn approves thoroughly of Krutch's Freudian life of Poe (1926). Poe, the victim of a "defense-neurosis," rationalizes "his own lack of passion, humanity, ethical perception..." (*SAL*, 157). Baudelaire, Poe's great advocate, shares these defects. While lambasting the aesthetic or decadent approaches of the French and American poets, Lewisohn takes the opportunity to hit tangentially the "intricate dullness of Mr. Joyce" and "the pornography of the late Mr. Lawrence." Such remarks do not lend the chapter credibility. He admires some of Poe's tales, to some degree, but thinks they have only a limited appeal.

Hawthorne, Lewisohn judges, was the most normal of the three, managing to free himself somewhat from withdrawal and guilt, from his "troubled and obscure and stripped and shivering soul." *The Scarlet Letter*, Hawthorne's masterpiece, is stamped with the mark of true tragedy; *The Blithedale Romance* is the "least spectral" of his works. His comments in letters and journals show shrewdness. Hawthorne, therefore, is a classic, though on shaky grounds. In his strictures on Hawthorne Lewisohn is indebted to a whole school of Hawthorne observers, from Montégut to Julien Green. He would have profited more from a closer study of Henry James's *Hawthorne* (1879), which saw the romancer as making the best possible use of limiting circumstances.

Most eccentric is Lewisohn's utter dismissal of Melville, especially since the renaissance of interest in Melville was already in progress, following the studies of Raymond Weaver and Lewis Mumford. Melville, he states, never attained "creative self-catharsis." In his constant flight from reality, "the world was a homeless and empty place and his soul cast out and orphaned." Melville was a "querulous man, a fretful man"; *Moby Dick*, when not merely sound and fury, is "inchoate and dull." Melville is not "even a minor master." Here Lewisohn must bear full responsibility for his absurdities. Although Lewisohn did not approve of transcendentalism, which did not grasp the tragic aspects of life, neither did he appreciate these romancers who conveyed the "power of darkness."

Book V, "Demos Speaks," concerned primarily with Abraham Lincoln, Walt Whitman, and Mark Twain—closer presumably to the American soil—is a much better chapter. His discussion of

Twain is good. He doesn't take seriously Brook's thesis that Twain's wife and puritanical influences damaged Twain's writing. Anticipating Bernard de Voto, Lewisohn stresses Twain's role as a folk artist, a voice of the West, best as a writer when close to his early experiences. Twain's shortcoming is that he had no philosophy, save for a village agnosticism, to meet the disillusionment of his later years. "He had nothing within wherewith to resist the late perception of human life as tragic." But Twain is the quintessential American, most valuable when writing out of memories of boyhood and adolescence. Lewisohn is oblivious, apparently, to such worthy later works as *Puddinhead Wilson* and "The Man Who Corrupted Hadleyburg." In total, however, his discussion of Twain is both appreciative and insightful.

Lewisohn's appraisal of Whitman needs some redress. True, he recognizes Whitman's poetic talent: "Walt Whitman—most strange and difficult figure in all our letters and perhaps the greatest, certainly the most far-reaching, far-echoing voice" (*SAL*, 198). For Lewisohn, as for other of his contemporaries, Whitman must be read in fragments, for he often writes drivel. More recent scholars, with considerable success, have studied whole poems by Whitman instead of fragments. Lewisohn bluntly speaks of Whitman's homosexuality, evidenced in the *Calamus* poems—still a matter of hush-hush and disagreement. Lewisohn affirms Whitman as a great, but flawed, artist. "America, in brief, has had to pay a heavy price for her most highly endowed poet being an unlettered man as well as a man of hopelessly eccentric personality" (*SAL*, 212). To the modern reader Whitman remains a great poet and does not seem so strange.

Book VI, "The Rise of the Novel," begins a discussion of Realism and Naturalism, where Lewisohn is on surer ground. On the minor novelists—Harriet Beecher Stowe, Sarah Orne Jewett, George Washington Cable, Mary Wilkins Freeman, and many others—he is very reliable. Of William Dean Howells, he wrote a judicious and extended appreciation, with which Oscar Cargill, long a professor of American Literature at New York University, was delighted, for Howells had been neglected or disaparaged in the 1920s. Lewisohn was not really a Jamesian, though he grants James the accolade of being "the most eminent man of letters America has to show." He likes most of James's short stories and novellas; in contrast, he refers to his later novels, including *The Wings of the Dove* and *The Ambassadors*, as "cathedrals of frosted glass." Despite his intellectual honesty, James—Lewisohn continues—was an old, prissy bachelor, engaged in flight (Lewisohn's condemnatory warhorse): "Flight was his motive; frustration was his theme; flight and frustration interwined was the figure in his carpet" (*SAL*, 260). James knew all that could be gained from "vigilance and sympathy," but withdrew from participation. Here again Lewisohn's judgment seems flawed, though he would probably have some modern sympathizers.

Lewisohn underestimates Stephen Crane, criticizes both William James's pragmatism and Santayana's alienation from American culture, and expresses a complete admiration for Emily Dickinson. His discussion of individual lines and poems by Dickinson reveals poetic sensitivity; so had his discussion of Emerson as poet. His analysis of Dreiser, psychological in approach, is a highlight in the book.

Book X, "The Great Cultural Debate," is an extended exposition of the Battle of the Books, with the Humanists on one side and the younger critics, led by Mencken, on the other. Ten years before, Lewisohn had aligned himself vehemently with the younger critics, but now correctly apprehended that he was closer to the Humanists than he had been. In this chapter, therefore, he draws a middle line: "More hates democracy on account of the exceeding wickedness of men's hearts; Mencken hates it no less on account of the exceeding thickness of their wits; More's ideal is a theocracy with clerical aristocrats as the rulers of mankind, Mencken's is an oligarchy of *Junkers* (*SAL*, 430).[3] Lewisohn pairs himself with Van Wyck Brooks as posing a *via media* in the debate, more aware than either side of the creative or biographical sources of art and less attuned to reactionary politics. Lewisohn, modifying the rebellious stance of *A Modern Book of*

Criticism (1919), sees himself, like Brooks, attempting to come to terms with American culture and celebrating its progressive tradition.

On contemporary writers, Lewisohn is erratic, to say the least. He favors the populists and realists, consequently praising those he believes belonged in this category, Carl Sandburg, Edgar Lee Masters, Robert Frost, Sherwood Anderson (though he calls Anderson sex-obsessed!), Sinclair Lewis, and Willa Cather, but disapproves of more involuted stylists and seemingly alienated writers, William Faulkner, Ezra Pound, T.S. Eliot, who have subsequently proven among the most challenging of twentieth-century writers. In all fairness to Lewisohn, his views were similar to those of other critics in the 1930s, e.g., Brooks, in his last volume of *Makers and Finders* (1955) and even in the young Alfred Kazin's *On Native Grounds* (1941).

Conclusion: Some reviewers praised *Expression in America* without reservation (Carl Van Doren, Joseph Wood Krutch); others (Granville Hicks, Howard Mumford Jones, Gilbert Seldes) thought the author's Freudian approach damaged an otherwise valuable work. True, Lewisohn's psychoanalytic approach hurt the work, especially in his chapters on Poe, Hawthorne, and Melville, but underlying his flawed psychoanalysis was something more disturbing: a concept of *reality* with which he could find many good writers wanting.

His concept of reality is twofold: first, the nitty-gritty, factual stuff of American life—Melville and Henry James are condemned for seeking an "escape" from such reality; second, a sound and well-rounded assessment of life, in Arnold's terms, a sound criticism of life—which, for Lewisohn had populist and democratic overtones. In different ways, the Puritans, Whitman, and Edith Wharton, illustrated a lack of "classic" qualities. By applying yardsticks to approaches to reality—as had the Humanists in an earlier period—Lewisohn did not permit writers to give free rein to imagination and to define *reality* in terms suitable to themselves. Lionel Trilling's essay, "Reality in America," in which Trilling examines Parrington's flaws in assessing reality, apply to Lewisohn as well. *Expression in America* has elements of greatness, but must be judged finally, applying Lewisohn's designation for Melville, as an "important curiosity."

Preface to Rank's *Art and Artist:* Turning from Freud

In his preface to *Art and Artist*, a selection from Otto Rank's writings on art translated from the German in 1932, Lewisohn sees Rank breaking new ground in discovering the sources of art. Rank abandons all approaches that seem indebted to nineteenth-century mechanism. Consequently, Lewisohn seems less sympathetic than he had been to Naturalism and Freudian principles, as they were commonly applied to literary criticism.

Freud had correctly shifted attention from the nineteenth-century view of a universe governed by scientific principles as the source of art to the human psyche; but even Freud had encouraged certain rigid concepts, thought Lewisohn, that owed their existence to nineteenth-century mechanism. One such concept was that art is the sublimation of sexual instincts, a view too partial to do justice to the total scope of man's creativity. Rank, on the other hand, sees man as the creator of his universe through art, myth, science, and religion. Rank based his conclusions on studies of anthropological and psychological materials; Ernst Cassirer, whom Lewisohn never mentions though his later statements bear similarities to Cassirer's, based his conclusions on neo-Kantian grounds.

To the reader of Lewisohn's work, the most significant implication of Lewisohn's preface is his unstated, but inevitable abandoment of the idea of the "Creative Eros" as the source of art—the idea upon which his short novel *The Golden Vase* was predicated. Lewisohn writes of Rank: "Thus he destroys the facile notion of art as a by-product of the sexual instinct."[4]

All art, Lewisohn asserts, is "creative and self-representative," a free spiritual activity tending to liberate the artist from the biological and material and from the collective culture of his age. The personality of the artist is autonomous, an example of man's ability to elevate himself to the level of vision.

The Magic Word: Homer, Shakespeare, Goethe

The Magic Word: Studies in the Nature of Poetry (1950), Lewisohn's last critical work, consists of an introduction, a chapter called "The Magic Word," which incorporates a theory of poetic diction, and separate chapters on Homer, Shakespeare, and Goethe. The section on Shakespeare is so wrong-headed it almost ruins the book.

The introduction states that poetry and literature originate in word and myth. Western criticism, which Lewisohn all too succinctly summarizes, has paid scant attention to the "word" or poetic diction. Exceptions, he continues, are the moderns Valéry and Rilke. "Is it not strange, since words are the materials of human expression, its very substance and texture, the stuff of which it is made, that no one apparently has sought the secret of the character of literature in *them*, in the nature of language itself and as such?"[5] Lewisohn implies a greater originality adhering to his discussion than is deserved. Certainly, in the nineteenth century "words" were not neglected. One thinks immediately of chapter 14 of *Biographia Literaria* (1817), in which Coleridge amends Wordworth's conception of poetic diction; of the section on language in Emerson's *Nature* (1836), which proffers a symbolic theory of expression; and of "The Hero as Poet," in *On Heroes, Hero-Worship, and the Heroic in History* (1840), in which Carlyle echoes much of what Lewisohn tries to communicate: the poet as the mythmaker of his age and the word as symbolic and musical vehicle. In dismissing his predecessors as nonexistent, Lewisohn was perfunctory and neglectful.

The second chapter, "The Magic Word," is better. Lewisohn cites the verses in *Genesis* that remind us that, though God created all living things, man was assigned the task of naming them—a kind of second creation. Man's first utterances were both the cry (*Anruf*) and the call (*Zuruf*), both exclamation and symbol. Archibald MacLeish's statement, therefore, that a "poem must not mean but be," is inaccurate; a poem both *is* and *means* simultaneously. Examining words for identical objects in different language families, Lewisohn concludes that these words are so disparate it is apparent that symbolic meanings outweigh the imitative in importance.

The French *symbolistes,* beginning with Mallarmé, demonstrated a heightened consciousness of words in poetry, but invented nothing new. Lewisohn praises Mallarmé, Valéry, and Rilke, but years had not softened his hostility to contemporary American poets: "Among Americans, the angry repudiation of this country, which set in with Ezra Pound—their tragic alienation, their spiritual homelessness, in both the world and the universe—produced the opaque and tortured and helplessly cacophonous work of the neo-esthetes from Wallace Stevens to, let us say, Delmore Schwartz" (*MW*, 17). Lewisohn has retained this damaging blind spot to the last.

Along with the "word" we find the "myth," which, resembling a dream, symbolically bodies forth a total picture of life. Myths express "the realities of the soul." In his discussion of myth Lewisohn often seems to adopt the commonplaces of the 1940s and 1950s that he found compatible with his own views. The successors to the great myths of the past have been reduced in scope in modern times because of the bleakness of our spiritual landscape. Myths cannot grow in the desperate "twilight region" of modern life.

The chapter on Homer is very good, not because it sets forth new ideas but because it states accepted ideas both thoughtfully and eloquently. What was often thought has rarely been so well expressed. Lewisohn begins by attacking the theory of the multiple authorship of the *Iliad* and the *Odyssey.* The theory of multiple authorship defies the creative unity evident in the Homeric epics, the singleness of vision characteristic of the work of art. Lewisohn aptly quotes Goethe on Friedrich Wolf, the first propounder of the theory. He examines Homer's two pictures of the poet-minstrel in the Odyssey, Phemios in Ithaca and Demodokos in Phaecia, both noble figures, divinely inspired.

Homer's diction is marked by "freshness of perception" and "closeness to things." Homer makes the world both luminous and delightful, and even if, in the *Iliad* particularly, he renders the bitter, the evil, and the barbaric, he delineates unpleasant actions against a background of a larger nature beautiful in itself and in its natural processes. "The world of Homer is luminous and fresh and entire" (*MW*, 44).

Homer's gods are "simply human beings who are strong, immortal, beautiful and above all law" (*MW*, 48). In contrast, Homer depicts human life with a dark, pagan pessimism; mortality renders life worthless, redeemed only by the loveliness of domestic affections, the tenderness with which Homer conveys family feeling. Lewisohn's comparison of gods and men in Homer seems incomplete. Because men are mortal, they alone are capable of heroism and tragedy; the gods are frequently only comic. Men, therefore, except in strength, are often more impressive than the gods. Achilles and Hector shed a brighter light than Ares and Apollo.

In Homer, Lewisohn concludes, diction and myth project "objectivity and detachment" and a delineation of "human action and passion against the background of the eternal and beautiful world" (*MW*, 43).

Lewisohn's chapter on Shakespeare attests to his critical independence it not his good judgment. He claims a kinship with eighteenth-century critics of Shakespeare, citing with approval not only Samuel Johnson but also Thomas Rymer (who had called *Othello* "a bloody farce") and Voltaire (who lamented Shakespeare's complete absence of good taste). Lewisohn even approves Milton's reference to Shakespeare's singing his "native woodland notes wild." The nineteenth-century critics, for Lewisohn, err this side of idolatry; of twentieth-century scholars, Lewisohn reveals complete ignorance; in any event, if he has read this more recent scholarship, he does not refer to it.

Shakespeare is the master of passionate or dramatic expression; otherwise, he has not much to offer, a "poet not sage, dreamer not thinker, unselfconscious genius in an unintellectual and fiery age" (*MW*, 84). The first to emerge from a "barbaric age," Shakespeare's language is "exuberant and abandoned." Inferior to Sophocles and Ibsen in dramatic form, he fills his stories with improbabilities. He has no "fixed wisdom or guided thought," the disorderly poet of an age marked by spiritual disorder. In reading Lewisohn, we seem to be turning back the clock more than two hundred years. Here is monumnental folly.

On Goethe, Lewisohn is on surer ground, immediately revealing a close sympathy and an intimate grasp of biographical detail and the poet's work. Employing as a springboard Valéry's speech on the centenary of Goethe's death in 1932, Lewisohn effectively does away with certain stereotypes Valéry holds about Goethe. Goethe was not a "monument of serenity," but one who hid his agitation with a rigid self-discipline, for which he paid severely. He was neither a voluptary (his relations with women were both subtler and sadder) nor a pagan: often anticlerical, he stated the human need for God, assurances of immortality, and virtue.

A sage, Goethe lived in a world losing faith and coherence of meaning. He stressed the autonomous personality, seeking freedom in responsibility. He substituted for the great poetic forms of the past more limited eighteenth-century forms, prizing clarity, sententiousness, epigrammatic quality. He is the poet of the modern.

The Magic Word, like *Expression in America,* is a work of mixed merit. The book displays extensive learning, though with serious lacunae, a fine use of poetic lines as touchstones (always one of Lewisohn's strengths), and a mature eloquence only occasionally marred by self-consciouness or the wish to dazzle. It presents Lewisohn entering new critical areas during the post-World War II period.

Chapter Six
The Polemicist:
No Mean Prophet
Lewisohn's Jewish Non-Fiction

Lewisohn's writings as polemicist include: *Israel* (1925), *The Permanent Horizon: A New Search for Old Truths* (1934), *The Answer* (1938), and *The American Jew: Character and Destiny* (1950). With the exception of *The Permanent Horizon*, these books argue against the inclinations of Jews to forget their Jewish identity and assimilate into their non-Jewish surroundings. In the United States, he asserted, a cultural pluralism should prevail, in which Jews can retain their own institutions and their character as a people. Just as blacks in later times have asserted that "black is beautiful," so Lewisohn pressed for a nonapologetic, forthright acceptance by Jews of their own character and destiny. Solomon Grayzel draws a legitimate distinction between Lewisohn's attitude in *Up Stream* and that exhibited in his later Jewish writings: "Lewisohn initially saw the situation in terms of thwarted ambition—the American Jew's burning desire to participate in the growth of America hurling itself vainly against the suspicions and prejudices of his non-Jewish neighbors—later he began to see that greater than the tragedy of Christian prejudice was the tragedy of the American Jew turning away from his own heritage."[1]

Also, beginning with *Israel* in 1925, Lewisohn was a fervent Zionist, advocating a Jewish state in Palestine. Stanley F. Chyet writes: "The *Jewish Post* eulogized Ludwig Lewisohn in 1956 as 'the first great American literary spokesman for the Zionist movement': that would have pleased him enormously."[2] Paradoxically, in *Israel*, he wished the Palestiniam state, since realized as Israel, to bear a multilingual, cultural diversity, to retain the cosmopolitanism and universal outlook Jews have often displayed in the past. He wished Jews to avoid a narrow, intense nationalism, which Lewisohn—from the time of World War I—indentified with xenophobia, militarism, and war. Similarly, in the United States Jews were to avoid assilimation but also study Western culture as a whole. Even in his most Jewish-minded phase Lewisohn did not set aside his own humanistic training and study.

In the mainstream of American literature Lewisohn's polemical writings might be regarded as parochial, but the problems of minorities remain of great concern to all Americans. Forced importations and liberal immigration policies have brought with them important subcultures from which Americans cannot avert their attention.

Certainly, many of Lewisohn's polemical pages remain eloquent and powerful, and many American Jews, now graying and growing older, think of themselves as in his debt. His influence did not extend, probably, to Jews already strongly committed to their religion, but to those with borderline commitments or to those acculturated to the American scene. He had made the transition himself from an almost complete assimilation to a strong sense of his own Jewish identity.

Lewisohn's best book of argument is the first—*Israel*, the title of which does not refer to the modern state, born in 1948, but to the whole range of Jewish life, to the House of Israel, as displayed in the United States, Germany and Austria, Poland, and Palestine in 1925. The book is one of travel and observation as well as argument, and descriptive details lend the volume a concreteness and objectivity sometimes lacking in his later work. Stanley Chyet calls it a "lovely, melodic, empyrean sort of book, the utterances of a man who had discovered in himself a love for the abraded contours of a land and an identity."[3]

Edward Sapir, the linguist, in a contemporary review of *Israel*, found it inferior to *Up Stream*, averring that the "fire of *Israel* owes much of its illumination and certainly much of its heat to the intense flame of a thwarted personal ambition."[4] Sapir continues that Lewisohn's bitterness against assimilation was the result of his own baffled inability to achieve serenity as a Jew in Western society. A similar complaint was also registered by H. L. Mencken, in his review of *Mid-Channel*: "The repatriated and reconditioned Jew . . . is still bound to be more or less uneasy."[5] To Sapir, Lewisohn's note of aggressive insistence indicated both a failure of philosophy and thwarted will. Sapir, also Jewish, thinks of the Jew as one whose peculiar function is that of the universal mediator, the critic, of the "cultural goods of all localisms" and as one who must achieve a personal synthesis of the disparate elements of his surroundings and traditions. In the controversies milling around Lewisohn in his lifetime, his critics have tended not to extend him his due credit because they have seen his ideas mainly as the outgrowth of psychological conflict.

Looking back from the 1980s, however, one recognizes Lewisohn's position as more valid that Sapir's. *Israel* seems almost prophetic, forecasting later events so well that one cannot interpret the work simply in terms of the author's personal and intellectual tumult. His chapters on Germany and Austria, where many prominent Jewish authors whom he met, including Jacob Wasserman, Stefan Zweig, and Arthur Schnitzler, were almost oblivious to their Jewish origins, accurately set the stage for the rise and dominance of Hitler. He writes: "Germany is the classical land of assimilation: it is the classical land of anti-semitism."[6] Lewisohn sees German-Jewish scholars and statesmen, relying on the always unreliable god of assimilation, unwilling to recognize the symptoms of a mounting and dangerous racism. He speaks of "the German reactionaries brooding over revenge" and "the bloody tyrants" of Poland. Hitler was already a force. The process of assimilation was proving bankrupt in Germany and could provide a parable to American Jews: " . . . assimilation is bankrupt. Germany was the great laboratory of the experiment. It was an inescapable part of the modern historic process. But the experiment has failed. It is not necessary that several American generations be sacrificed to foreknown humiliation and predictable disasters" (I, 79-80).

The author had traveled a long distance from certain pro-German attitudes he had held before and during World War I. As a contrast to Wasserman and others, Lewisohn chose later to translate from the German thirteen stories by Jacob Picard under the title *The Marked One and Other Stories* (1956), with an unusually fine introduction by the translator. *The Marked One* recorded life in certain pockets of South and Southwest Germany in which Jews had maintained their distinction; these fragmented communities, of course, have now been completely obliterated. Picard, unlike many Jewish writers in Germany, described Jews not totally absorbed by their surrounding culture. Lewisohn's introduction reads: "Jacob Picard has strongly, tenderly, beautifully rescued from a probable oblivion an entire world of our people and has added this community both to the realm of history and of the human imagination."[7]

Chapter 3, "House of Bondage," in *Israel* contains some of the best writing in the book, a masterly description of Jewish life and places in Poland. Always evident are unspeakable poverty and oppression. Vilna, the center of Jewish learning, was "huddled, desolate, medieval." Of Jewish schools in Vilna, he writes: "In spite of the minority rights guaranteed by the Western nations that established the Polish republic, none of these schools receive any state aid, although sixty percent of all urban taxes are paid by Jews" (I, 104–5). Nevertheless, Polish Jews showed a greater sense of identity and dignity than their Western counterparts. "No American," Edward Sapir—Lewisohn's critic—comments, "after reading Mr. Lewisohn's book, can continue to feel that the uncouth Jewish immigrant from Poland and Lithuania comes to this land as a spiritual mendicant."[8] The Eastern European Jew still maintained his Jewish way of life and traditions of learning.

Intolerable conditions drove thousands of Jews weekly to seek escape from Poland, to Palestine and elsewhere. The gates to the United States were closed in 1924. In his enthusiastic chapters on Jewish Palestine, Lewisohn mixes factual information and description with his idealist hopes for the future. In Palestine Jews could be themselves without constraint: "The virtue of Tel Aviv is that Jews can be noisy there without hesitation." Jewish Palestine was small and poor, but the pioneers worked hard, with a sense of promise: "A small land and a poor land. Yet not so poor but that it can harbor a few million of our people; not so small or so poor but that, as in ancient days, it can give birth to ideas that mankind will not willingly let die...." He sees Jewish Palestine as having its own separate mission: culture, pacifism, democracy, unity among Jews. Palestine, or Israel, would be a new type of state. Extending gratuitously to most Jews his own ideals, "The great majority of Jews," he writes, "are liberal, pacific, humanitarian" (*I*, 277). Again, he writes: "The House of Jacob is remembering its necessary service to mankind—to resist unrighteousness, to break every yoke, to re-establish peace." To Lewisohn, the Jew's goal was not to be knightly in the "Nordic, pagan, belligerent" sense. Such feudal ideals had brought havoc to Europe, as he was to relate at greater length in *Cities and Men*. Lewisohn did not foresee the practical problems of modern Israel, the need for effective military forces and a huge defense budget, the warfare with Arab nations, the social and economic problems that bedevil it as well as other nations. Here he is less prescient than in his chapters on Germany; yet he saw the necessity of a Jewish Palestine and pressed its claims upon his readers.

In later years, as columnist and editor, Lewisohn was to advocate, as did others, a secular, bi-national state and society, in which Palestinian Arabs enjoyed the same rights and privileges as Jews; such a state would evolve under British sponsorship. But the British Mandate proved a failure, and the distresses of Jews in Europe, the lack of willingness on the part of the United States and other Western countries, as manifested in the Evian Conference, to assist Jews trying to escape Hitler's Europe, led Lewisohn to adopt a more militant posture, setting aside the idea of a bi-national state.[9] He tended to see World War II and the concentration camps as a breakdown of Christianity, a disruption which confirmed his idea of the Jew as the redeeming agent in Western civilization. In this regard, Lewisohn placed too great a burden on Jews, who had enough to do to live and to accomplish their own physical and spiritual salvation without saving the rest of the world as well.

The Permanent Horizon: A New Search for Old Truths (1934), written during the Depression, is a lesser work than *Israel*, without the earlier work's wealth of particularities. But time has not invalidated its premises. Europe, Lewisohn writes, is in darkness: America itself, in danger. Desperate political philosophies, whether of the right or the left, born of modern inquietude, have been proposed as remedies; Lewisohn defends the "classical" or "permanent" man and opposes the economic determinists "who cannot beat the notion that the soul is dynamic and that the dynamic or creative quality of the individual soul is the same force that has given birth to myth and religion and art."[10]

The middle class, on the defensive, still remains the best social hope of mankind. "The bourgeois desires security, dignity, privacy, liberation from sordid care for the sake of cultural disinterestedness. If he does not desire the last for himself, he desires it or, at least in many cases, creates it for his children" (PH, 32).[11] (Here Lewisohn manifests a conservatism not present in his anti-bourgeois position in Up Stream, a decade earlier.) Marx's vision in Das Kapital "is the flight into Utopia of a doubly homeless and spiritually disinherited bourgeois" (PH, 34). The old moralities and myths are still potent; the ends of society and men are unchanging, not to be abandoned for some heady extreme: "Historic-minded, non-Utopian thinking is the first duty of the hour and age" (PH, 88). Fascism is a retreat into barbarism.

Lewisohn's conservatism still seems meritorious at the present, when the violent social philosophies of his time have lost credibility in much of the Western world.

One might briefly mention here the anthology Rebirth: A Book of Modern Jewish Thought that Lewisohn assembled in 1935. The title points to the motif of the collection, the return to Judaism of various prominent persons, including Buber and Franz Rosenzweig. A representative modern serving Lewisohn's purpose is described in the preface:

"Take the fragments that I have selected and translated from Bernard Lazare's Le Fumier de Job. Lazare, who was born in Nîmes...considered himself to be and felt himself to be a Latin, a Frenchman of the South. Then came the accusation and the trial and the condemnation of

Dreyfus, and Lazare turned in upon himself and found the substance of the Jewish soul and without much help or instruction from anyone...."[12]

As early as 1935 the introduction states a theme Lewisohn will subsequently never relinquish: the Jew who reintegrates with his people is "helping to save not only Israel, but a world pagan and unredeemed."[13]

Of special interest, in the autobiographical sketch Lewisohn draws for this anthology, is his designation of the 1920s as a period when he was "confused and misled...alienated from his people";[14] except for *The Case of Mr. Crump* (which he must have judged too good to renounce) and *The Golden Vase* (which he always overestimated), he renounces all his work on non-Jewish subjects. The reader does well to disregard such disavowals, which are not unusual in literary history, from Chaucer's redaction to *The Canterbury Tales* to Tolstoy's *What Is Art?*

A similarly polemical anthology that Lewisohn put together was *Among the Nations* (1948), with works by Mann, Maugham, Galsworthy, and Lacretelle—sympathetic non-Jewish writers pointing up the bankruptcy of Jewish assimilation. These works, three tales and a play, are striking for their literary value.

The Answer—The Jew and the World: Past, Present and Future (1939) is a collection of columns syndicated for Jewish readers. Although the numerous individual selections constitute a superior group of popular journalistic pieces, they suffer in book form from redundancy, amplifications of the obvious, and paucity of leading ideas. The volume blends the valuable and the inconsequential. One might summarize that the answer referred to in the title is that the Jew must proudly assume his identity—a perennial answer that transcends particular times. Lewisohn deplores the Jewish liberal's forgetting his Jewishness, the Jewish communist's hatred of it. The history of Judaism since the Enlightenment consists of a string of false allurements seducing the Jew from his separate character and destiny. In an autobiographical passage of interest in the final chapter Lewisohn states that his "identification with my people and my embracing with all my heart and strength of the Zionist cause" has isolated him as

an American man of letters. Others say of him: "Oh, he's gone so
Jewish, you know...."[15] But he declares the inevitability and
rightness of his choice, though he has lost income and reputation.

The American Jew: Character and Destiny (1950) is a more
tightly knit work, a guide to the perplexed among American Jews.
The work repeats, in more organic and eloquent form, the arguments of *The Answer*, with a greater stress on the need for and
practices of traditional religion. It represents, as compared to *The
Answer*, a greater swing toward religious orthodoxy. The preface
contains a valuable summing-up of his past polemical writing,
revealing both truthful assessment and a mingled self-pity and
self-congratulation:

When in 1925 I published *Israel*, the first American Zionist book on
that scale, and predicted the imminent danger in Central Europe and
emphasized the recolonization of Palestine as the single hope of the
Jewish people, I was called a paranoiac; when in 1934 I published *The
Permanent Horizon*, I was called a reactionary — because I pleaded in
defense of the classical form of human life against the forces of disintegration; when in a novel *Trumpet of Jubilee* in 1937 I pointed out the
accursed identity of the Nazi and Soviet systems I was not believed; I
was accused of the grossest partisanship. Today all that I pleaded for in
those years is accepted and known.[16]

In the same preface, along with an appeal to a return to traditional Judaism, he acknowledged debts to Nicholas Berdyaev,
Karl Barth, and Reinhold Niebuhr.

Jews have always been the target of anti-Semitism, the book
argues, because they represent in their traditions certain spiritual
values other peoples in the world are not always ready to accept,
though these values are necessary for their redemption as well;
Jews have themselves, since the promises of the Emancipation,
forgotten their own mission: "It was forgotten that the Jews had
been hated and resisted precisely because they had brought with
them into the world a universal challenge—the challenge of God,
of peace, of righteousness, but they could no longer issue that
challenge if they abandoned themselves and their ways and their
sanctification of life."[17]

The passion for peace, for sound justice, for democracy must turn the Jew toward Zionism and orthodoxy. In *The American Jew* Lewisohn identifies the humanistic values he had cultivated all his life—his pacificism in the First World War, his rebellion against American materialism and Babbittry in the early 1920s, his battle against irrational social forces in the 1930s—with religious orthodoxy. The book marks the culmination of his gradual drift toward religion.

Another eloquent, though briefer, expression of Lewisohn's last and most religious position is his introduction, called "The Jew and the Book," to the anthology *The Great Jewish Books*, edited by Samuel Caplan and Harold U. Ribalow (1952). It was probably Muhammed, states Lewisohn, who first addressed Jews as "The People of the Book." Until a later age Jews did not have to think of themselves as such. They needed no reminders that they were bound to the Bible. The giving and the receiving of the Book was the historic event that turned Jews into Jews. The Book was not only scripture; it was literature, brimming with life and written with art: "Full-grown, mature, this sublime and soaring, this stern and lapidary style of saying and chanting...sprung from the midst of Israel."[18]

The biblical text demanded universal literacy among Jews, a rapt attention and devotion to study. But the spirit of nihilism in modern life has affected Jews as well as others; the authentic Jewish books have often been left bleak and alone. "But there are signs here and there that the embers are glowing and that a flame may yet again spring forth."[19]

Herzl and Lewisohn

In 1955, the year of his death, Lewisohn edited selected writings by Theodor Herzl, the father of modern Zionism, in a volume called *Theodor Herzl: A Portrait for This Age*. The book appeared with a preface, highly appreciative of Herzl, by David Ben Gurion, first prime minister of Israel, and with an introduction of seventy-two pages—a monograph both detailed and precise—by Lewisohn.

What may at first seem odd is that Lewisohn includes in this reader a collection of Herzl's undistinguished *feuilletons* and dramatic sketches, written during Herzl's first phase as journalist, as well as his later, more significant Zionist tracts. The selection conforms to Lewisohn's purpose—to render a psychological protrait of Herzl in his times. Lewisohn's was an exercise in what today is called psychohistory. Herzl's life marks an intersection of paths: the course of Jewish history since the French Revolution and the development of modern Zionism.

Lewisohn's monograph first analyzes the impact of the Enlightenment and the French Revolution, which encouraged the granting of equal and civil rights to Jews with the proviso that Jews forget the "irregularities" of their religion and merge freely with other citizens; differences were to be suppressed in the adoption of a common posture among Western Europeans. Many Jews in France, Germany, and Austria hastened to assimilate, and non-Jews cooperated in this process. Of course, in Eastern Europe, where the Enlightenment did not penetrate to the same extent, Jews kept apart from the rest of the community and, in ghettos, maintained their ancient traditions.

Despite the assimilative patterns of the nineteenth century, including intermarriage, the attempt to eradicate ancient differences, in Lewisohn's opinion, proved a failure. Jews either found internal reasons to prevent the shedding of their identities or encountered external barriers blocking assimilation and secular advancement. In a century when Christian, as well as Jewish, faith diminished, anti-Semitism shifted grounds from the religious to the racial and the economic. The most startling evidence of anti-Semitism, to Herzl as well as innumerable others, was the Dreyfus Affair, in the 1890s, in which an assimilated Jewish officer in the French army was conspiratorially accused of treason and sent to Devil's Island. Much of this material Lewisohn had fictionalized in *Renegade*, with its backdrop of the Enlightenment in France, his best novel written after *The Island Within*.

Theodor Herzl (1860–1904) exemplified the failure of assimilation and the adoption of a new Zionist idea. A Hungarian journalist, raised in a German-speaking culture, he had little knowledge of Judaism; he began the study of Hebrew at the end of his life. His devotion to religion was, for all practical purposes, non existent. Yet he was, after a kind of conversion or return, to give all his energy, time, and talent to Zionism, and he galvanized, in eight short years—from the time of the publication of the *Judenstaat* [The Jewish State] until his death—many European and American Jews to the acceptance of the ideals and programs of action that he propounded.

An only child, Herzl was boundlessly admired by his parents, especially by his mother, who built up in him exorbitant hopes for his future. This parental indulgence "hampered his maturing and crippled his judgment both of the world and of himself. He seemed to himself a prince in exile, unknown, unloved, unvalued."[20] The brilliant success he awaited did not arrive, and he took his revenge upon the world, in his *feuilletons*, with a display of harsh cynicism. He remained, despite hard effort, "merely a not quite topranking journalist and a mediocre playwright."[21]

This pattern of paternal or maternal ambition, followed by greater or lesser filial success, has repeated itself, Lewisohn continues, in thousands of Jewish families before and after Herzl. In periods of false emancipation success in one's career has proven a Jewish form of compensation for an uneasy position in society. (Lewisohn did not live to read Philip Roth's attack upon the "Jewish mother" in *Portnoy's Complaint*; one suspects he might have sympathized with Portnoy's dilemma, but extended at least equal sympathy to Portnoy's parents.) In America the son must be a doctor or lawyer; in central Europe, in an earlier time, the son had to be a professor, a writer, or an artist.

When his awakening came to Herzl, a sense of the futility of the aspirations of his co-religionists, his "repressed hurts and sorrows as a Jew, leaped into consciousness."[22] What psychology cannot explain is the sudden eruption into genius; Herzl, in his return to Judaism, soared far above average, displaying both greatness and consecration. "Therefore, despite his obvious weaknesses and the cultivation of the grandiose gesture, Herzl radiated in those years of burning and self-consuming an indescribable influence upon all who knew, saw, heard him...."[23]

What strikes the reader, in this psychological profile of Herzl, is that Lewisohn draws almost a mirror image of himself. To what extent Lewisohn was aware of these similarities is hard to say, though it seems impossible that he was totally oblivious of them. Raised in a non-Jewish setting, encouraged by his parents, and indulged, especially by his mother, in his desire for an academic and literary career, Lewisohn undertook, perhaps with excessive expectations, a course of literary training, to become a scholar and artist. His failure as a graduate student to find employment, which he attributed upon good evidence to his being a Jew, released in him a latent hostility to his American surroundings, parallel to Herzl's cynical response to the secular world around him. Lewisohn's sheltered youth, also, had not prepared him for the world around him, a lack he tried to repair by the study of Naturalistic writers, both German and American. Such overprotectiveness, he often stated, moreover, led to his disastrous first marriage.

Edmund Wilson's theory of the wound and the bow, of a psychic trauma leading to creative energy, applies to Lewisohn. The psychic blow suffered at Columbia University led to his best autobiography, *Up Stream*. The marriage contracted without adult preparation and knowledge led to *The Case of Mr. Crump*, perhaps his best novel, a painful, relentless, and moving picture of marital discord; and his sense that as a Jew he had been sidetracked out of his normal course led to *The Island Within*, an ironic and penetrating novel of several generations of Jews who have suffered deracination. Eventually, like Herzl, he was to turn, also, to a large extent, from literature to Jewish causes, including Zionism. Through his spiritual wanderings an early idealism, incorporated in his childhood, wove itself.

Lewisohn saw Herzl as a mediocre journalist and man of letters transformed into an extraordinary publicist, advocate, and ideologist. In this regard, Lewisohn and Herzl are not comparable. Lewisohn was more than a mediocre man of letters; he was the author of two fine novels, a memorable autobiography, and much good criticism, including that emanating from the drama desk at the *Nation* and the wider dimensions of *Cities and Men*.

As an advocate of Jewish causes, he did yeomanlike, often farsighted service, though without Herzl's brilliance. Herzl will be remembered as the founder of Zionism; Lewisohn, for a distinguished contribution to American literature.

After long deliberation and without the desire to exaggerate, one must conclude that Lewisohn, despite frequent foolishness, frenzy, and failure, has had the most significant career of any American Jewish man of letters. He painfully and self-consciously prepared the path that others could follow more easily. In the course of American Jewish letters, spanning writers from Abraham Cahan and even earlier forerunners to Bellow and Malamud, Lewisohn's work marks a turning point, rejecting the patterns of self-negation and the obliteration of the Jewish past that subsequent writers, following Lewisohn, could no longer accept.

Chapter Seven
Final Assessment

The question is: what place does Lewisohn hold in American literature? How has he been and how should he be appraised? C. Hugh Holman, a respected scholar, has referred to him as an "unjustly neglected" figure.[1] The bibliographical section on Lewisohn in *Literary History of the United States* concludes that scholarly articles on Lewisohn are "negligible."[2] That these statements are at least partially true is confirmed by the fact that this present account is the first full-length published study since Gillis (1933). The decline in his reputation below his worth can be attributed to the publicity (to which Lewisohn contributed) given to his marital entanglements and to his reversion—unwelcome in many quarters—to Judaism. The picture may not be as bleak as Holman and the *Literary History* suggest, but certainly his writings deserve more intense study.

A major problem in appraising him is that there were several Lewisohns. In his abundant, sometimes prolix, output over many years his interests are revealed as multifaceted and seemingly discontinuous. There was Lewisohn the scholar and translator; also, the Naturalist writer, the drama critic, the critic of several literatures, the aggressive Zionist and *ba'al tshuvah* (one who returns to Judaism), the author of autobiographies. Critical attention has been splintered, each commentator seeing Lewisohn only in the area of his own vision.

Autobiography and Fiction

Of his three autobiographical volumes, *Up Stream*, the first, remains untarnished. This work, which first brought Lewisohn national attention and general praise, except for those who saw it as "alien" (a term intermittently applied to all Lewisohn's work, especially by S. P. Sherman and Dorothea Brande), is still highly regarded. So good a critic as Geoffrey H. Hartman in 1980 refers to it as "remarkable." Writing of Randolph Bourne, a critic of Lewisohn's camp in the 1920s against the Humanists, Hartman states: "His counter-ideal of a 'trans-national America' that would no longer equate Americanization and assimilation, was echoed by Lewisohn in his remarkable autobiography *Up Stream* (1922.)"[3] *Up Stream* reversed the trend expressed by Mary Antin, who, in her autobiography *The Promised Land* (1912), advocated the complete assimilation of American Jews, and Lewisohn's book encouraged Anzia Yezierska and other Jewish writers to assert their own ethnic identity.

Lewisohn's succeeding volumes of autobiography, *Mid-Channel* and *Haven*, though indispensable today for our knowledge of his later years and thought, have inflicted upon his reputation much damage. By defending his turbulent personal life he threw wood on the fire. Of *Mid-Channel* (1929), H. L. Mencken, in his review, gently and ruefully expressed the wish that Lewisohn had not dealt so extensively with his personal affairs. To Mencken, Lewisohn's return to Jewishness was a proper subject for autobiography; it made good sense that a Jew, for his own peace of mind, proclaim himself a Jew; however, Lewisohn's aggressiveness, Mencken thought, bespoke the fact that he was not entirely at ease in Zion.[4] Elsewhere, Mencken referred to him as the "amiable" Dr. Lewisohn, as mild-mannered a Jew as ever "singed a Christian."

Less sympathetic reviewers found further evidence in Lewisohn's candid revelations that he was a "case," carrying over the tensions of his personal life into literature. Much of Lewisohn criticism is a matter of looking forward and backward in his career using these autobiographies as a fulcrum.

Among students of American Jewish fiction, *The Island Within*, among his novels, has stirred the most interest. However, upon publication, *The Island Within*, met with favorable reviews among readers of all backgrounds; what cavils were expressed were about specific points rather than general. How does one account, therefore, for so hostile an assessment more recently of the novel by Leslie Fiedler?

Fiedler termed the novel a "blending of self-pity and editorial." As late as 1971, Fiedler repeated, referring to Lewisohn and Ben Hecht, that "there is a real pathos in the efforts of the Jewish intellectual to see himself as Don Juan, an essential vanity in his striving to embody current themes of sexual freedom."[5] Lewisohn's only subject, Fiedler continues, was his own sex problems desperately projected as typical. Of the protagonist of the novel, Arthur Levy, Fiedler writes: "the sensitive Jew, a psychologist this time, still struggles with the *shikse* ... for the possession of his own soul"; Levy affirmed "a battered Romantic faith in sexual passion with an equally Romantic commitment to Zionism."[6]

Fiedler continues the tradition, begun in the 1920s, of labeling Lewisohn a "case," possibly deriving images from the two later autobiographies. Happily for this good *roman à thèse*, other critics have judged *The Island Within* more favorably, reverting in spirit to the reception accorded it upon publication. Bernard Sherman, in *The Invention of the Jew* (1969), mentions that *The Island Within* ran to thirty printings and has proven to be "one of th landmarks of Jewish-American fiction."[7] Allen Guttman, in *The Jewish Writer in America* (1971), refers to it as a "most significant book," adding that "the argument for peoplehood has never been more persuasively presented."[8] Harold U. Ribalow, Daniel Walden, and Stanley F. Chyet have commented on its present-day relevance and enduring appeal. All these testify to the fact that, if one reads *The Island Within* without preconceived ideas, one should find the novel still highly charged and meaningful.

Alas, Lewisohn's equally good, perhaps better, novel, *The Case of Mr. Crump* (1925), has received much less attention. Almost entirely autobiographical, it transcends its origins to become a powerful work of Naturalistic art. Despite the superlative reviews at its publication, with the occasional demur that its power verged on the "ugly," it has been almost forgotten. Because it has no ostensible Jewish content, it has escaped the scrutiny of those interested in American-Jewish fiction. It is true that Howard Mumford Jones and Richard Ludwig, in their fourth edition of *Guide to American Literature and Its Backgrounds since 1890* list *Mr. Crump*, along with works by Conrad Aiken, Maxwell Bodenheim, William Faulkner, F. Scott Fitzgerald, Waldo Frank, and Thomas Wolfe, as examples of striking "New Fiction."[9] But, though the Fourth Edition appeared in 1972, the list had apparently not been updated for many years. *Mr. Crump* certainly deserves better than its present oblivion. After Dreiser's best work, it stands among the best Naturalistic novels in American fiction.

Criticism

Of Lewisohn's copious criticism, the key critical estimate is Alfred Kazin's, in his chapter "Liberals and New Humanists" in *On Native Grounds* (1942).[10] In an extended footnote Kazin praises Lewisohn's scholarly work before coming to the *Nation*: his book on modern European drama, his printed lectures on modern German literature, his volume on French poetry, and his "valuable" early anthology, *A Modern Book of Criticism* (1919).[11] Kazin then especially commends *The Drama and the Stage*: "It is in *The Drama and the Stage*, a selection from his drama reviews published in the *Nation*, that Lewisohn's exciting contribution to the postwar renaissance is seen at its best."[12]

In Lewisohn's first phase as a critic, when he seemed the standard-bearer of the liberal critics, including Mencken, Randolph Bourne, Van Wyck Brooks, among others, Lewisohn proved "a force for progress." But his tendency to introduce the tensions of his personal life into his novels intruded itself into his criticism as well. "In practice, for all contempt for impressionism and the empirical methods of most American critics, he began more and more to write the history of literature as the history of Ludwig Lewisohn."[13] This process achieved its climax in his *Expression in America* (1932). Unhistorical in its approach, this history of American literature substituted Lewisohn's subjective judgments, derived from his personal projections and needs, for a more sober and considered appraisal. Lewisohn was a "frenzied apostle" who "carried the postwar discovery of sex and the calumny of the past to the point of self-ridicule."[14]

Essentially, Kazin's outline seems accurate. Lewisohn was most valuable as critic when most objective, and most flawed when most subjective. But one can bring certain reservations to Kazin's analysis. Since he praises everything Lewisohn wrote before *Expression in America*, ignoring *Cities and Men*, it seems apparent that his objections to Lewisohn stem from one book, the history of American literature with its dubious Freudianism and its finding Puritanism behind every door. Kazin's legitimate dislike of much of *Expression in America* colors everything he writes about Lewisohn before that work, praising with one hand and withdrawing with the other.

Just as *The Island Within* remains Lewisohn's best remembered, still controversial, novel, so, too, does *Expression in America* dominate recent discussion of his criticism. One cannot defend the critical work so heartily as the novel. Most commentators remember his Freudian debunking of Emerson, Thoreau, Melville, and Poe, his excessive castigation of Puritanism, and his discovering of Puritanism at the root of diverse phenomena. Of American criticism in the 1930s, C. Hugh Holman writes: "... the best known and most influential critical work employing the interpretation of Freud's ideas was Ludwig Lewisohn's *Expression in America* (1932), which established the sexual life or inhibition of the writer...as a standard for literary excellence."[15] At the same time these critics concede his excellent judgments and splendid passages when not engaged in promoting his prejudices.

Jay B. Hubbell, in his *Who Are the Major American Writers?* (1972), writes; "When his judgment was not distorted by prejudice, he could write excellent criticism; but his prejudices were many and unyielding."[16] Hubbell's book is valuable beyond his quest to ascertain the major American writers. It studies past histories of American literature and judgments in detail, a pursuit which points to an astonishing diversity of opinion. It reconciles one somewhat to Lewisohn's own lapses of judgment. But Hubbell correctly states that the book cannot be seen today as it appeared to many of its readers in 1932, when it was reviewed with great éclat. Carl Van Doren thought it "about the finest volume of American criticism produced to date." Perhaps the contemporary reviewer who saw it best was Howard Mumford Jones, in the *Yale Review* (Summer 1932): "Mr. Lewisohn is trying to write two books at one. One is a history of American literature, and the other is about sex and art...the two are inextricably confused....Mr. Lewisohn is at his best when forgetting Freud and forgetting his crochets, he confines himself to criticism of the old-fashioned sort...."

One section of *Expression in America* traditionally praised is Lewisohn's account of the Battle of the Books, the Ancients and the Moderns (in brief, More vs. Mencken.) Edgar Kemmler, in *The Irreverent Mr. Mencken* (1950), calls it "a full and inspired account of this battle." Kazin, Cargill, Hubbell, and John H. Raleigh express similar sentiments. Of course, Lewisohn had strayed from the "moderns" by 1932.

Carl Van Doren, an excellent critic and scholar, was always appreciative of Lewisohn as a critic. In his memoir *Three Worlds* (1936), he writes of Lewisohn: "He touched nothing that he did not elevate....Disciplined by learning, his mind kept a Goethean serenity when he wrote about literature."[17] Certain phrases become hereditary. Henri Peyre, in his important *Failures of Criticism* (1967), writes: "Critical talents have abounded since 1900: Mencken, George Jean Nathan, Carl Van Doren, Ludwig Lewisohn in his *serene and Goethean* moods; all have loved and served literature"[18] (Italics mine).

Probably the critical work that stirred the most controversy in its time and that, next to *Expression in America*, has thus provoked the most interest today is, surprisingly, Lewisohn's anthology *A Modern Book of Criticism* (1919), especially his slim "Introduction" to the volume. The book raised a battle cry against the Humanists. Marshall van Deusen writes (1975): "Ludwig Lewisohn, for one, whose social concerns came to full flower in the Romantic Freudianism of *Expression in America* (1932), described in the 'Introduction' to his anthology, *A Modern Book of Criticism*, his sense of crisis and of More's responsibility for it."[19]

Stuart P. Sherman, in *Americans* (1922), took up the gauntlet on behalf of the Humanists most forcefully. He quotes from the "Introduction" Lewisohn's egregious statement on the Moderns:

"Like a group of shivering young Davids—slim and frail but with a glimpse of morning sunshine on their foreheads—they face an army of Goliaths." Sherman comments: "The slim and shivering young Davids turn out on investigation to be Mr. Huneker, Mr. Spingarn, Mr. Mencken, Mr. Lewisohn, Mr. Hackett, Mr. Van Wyck Brooks, and Randolph Bourne." Sherman calls these "alien-minded" critics "restless impressionists, almost destitute of doctrine."[20]

Perhaps it is enough defense of the "young Davids" that they made modern literature, especially works of realism and Naturalism, more acceptable to the public, that they broke ground against prudery and the genteel tradition, and that they tried to relate literature to modern science. Vernon Parrington states that they rejected "Puritanical reticence and smug respectability."[21] But that the battling Moderns gave birth to no sustaining creed, that they were, as Sherman writes, "almost destitute of doctrine," has been echoed on several occasions, most recently by Geoffrey H. Hartman, in his *Criticism in the Wilderness: The Study of Literature Today* (1980). Hartman notes that T. S. Eliot's "Tradition and the Individual Talent" and Lewisohn's *A Modern Book of Criticism* appeared in the same year. Eliot stressed the importance of tradition for the man of letters; Lewisohn, in accents vaguely reminiscent of Emerson and Shelley, called upon the man of letters to be a prophet, attuned to the breezes of the future. Eliot's laconic style, Hartman continues, has worn better than Lewisohn's flamboyance; further, though Hartman declares his sympathies are strongly with Lewisohn's more democratic ideas, Eliot's classicism has provided his followers with a more enduring creed.

One can draw another parallel between Eliot and Lewisohn. Both felt in the 1920s a decline in modern values, a lack of a rational order in society and culture to sustain the individual. Eliot's turn to Anglicanism reenforced Eliot's adoption of a central tradition in English letters; it provided him with further links to Samuel Johnson and Lancelot Andrews. On the other hand, Lewisohn saw Christianity as partly responsible for the breakdown in modern man's search for peace and stability. Lewisohn's turn to Judaism and Zionism, in a sense, divorced him from critical predecessors, English or American. When he came to write *Expression in America*, his critical equipment was an eclectic mixture of Freud, Matthew Arnold, and the example of Thomas Mann.

Regrettably, *Cities and Men* (1928), like *Mr. Crump*, is overlooked today. The book is devoid of the flawed Freudianism critics have rightly objected to in *Expression in America*, yet it bears the critical maturity of the best passages of the later work. Without the vatic and propagandistic tenor of *A Modern Book of Criticism*, the various essays, eclectic in subject matter, are bound together by the author's attempt to counter the threat he felt in Europe to civilized life and standards. In letters Lewisohn seeks protection, whether in the nineteenth-century rational tradition of John Morley or in the religious currents of the twentieth century represented by Rilke and Buber, against an imminent downfall. The book represents a balanced critical Humanism Lewisohn could not always sustain.

Judaism and Zionism

Lewisohn's return to Judaism and his advocacy of Zionism, his ardent involvement with both over thirty years, demands a separate book. (Stanley F. Chyet's examination, "Lewisohn, a Zionist," published in Tel Aviv, is the most thorough thus far.) When Lewisohn first became involved in these currents, many must have felt he had fallen off a cliff into these waters. He seemed to have adopted an ideology mystifying for a man of letters. In the 1920s many American Jews, like other Americans, were complacent in their material success and their station in life, or they were caught up in the economic difficulties of the Depression. Many American Jews were ignorant of Palestine or indifferent to it. As with other Americans, Zionism seemed merely a chimera. Many Americans were apathetic about events in Germany and isolationist in foreign affairs. To intellectuals the Soviet Union seemed more attractive than threatening—until the Moscow purges of 1937. A Marxist critic, Bernard Smith, wrote in 1939:

"[Judaism] is Lewisohn's faith today and it is a thoroughly reactionary one, as can be seen in his rancorous gibes at every expression of collectivism."[22] Such an assessment must have been creditable to many at the time.

Maxwell Geismar wrote: "The ordinary mark of a first-rank author is that his writing is generally in some degree ahead of its time."[23] In his writings about Judaism and Zionism Lewisohn was, in some degree, ahead of his time. He took seriously the trends of Jewish history in the earlier twentieth century when others, including Jewish men of letters, did not. Today all Americans, perhaps all the world, are forced to confront, whether they want to or not, the terrors of the Holocaust, the existence of Israel, the Gulag Archipelago. Many Jews are in Lewisohn's debt; perhaps his intense and continued concern was rewarded with some degree of security that his religion had to offer him.

Notes and References

Preface

1. Leslie Fiedler, "The Jew in the American Novel," *Collected Essays* (New York, 1971), 2:79-81.
2. Analyticus (James W. Wise). *Jews Are Like That!* (New York, 1928), p. 109.
3. David Eckerling, "The Case of Ludwig Lewisohn," *Reflex* 5 (September, 1929):14-20.
4. Louis J. Bragman, "The Case of Ludwig Lewisohn," *American Journal of Psychiatry II* (September, 1931):319-33.
5. Milton Hindus, "Ludwig Lewisohn: From Assimilation to Zionism," *Jewish Frontier 31* (February, 1964):22-31.

Chapter One

1. Lewisohn's year of birth is given variously as 1882 or 1883. The date I have assumed is that used by Stanley F. Chyet, who is interested in Lewisohn biography. See Chyet, "Ludwig Lewisohn: The Years of Becoming," *American Jewish Archives* 11 (1959):125-47.
2. Ludwig Lewisohn, *Up Stream* (New York, 1922), p. 8; hereafter cited in text as *Up* followed by page number.
3. Bragman, "The Case of Ludwig Lewisohn," p. 320.
4. C. Hugh Holman describes this essay, "Books We Have Made," as follows: "valuable but not always accurate history of South Carolina writers," in *Bibliographical Guide to the Study of Southern Literature*, ed., Louis D. Rubin, Jr. (Baton Rouge: Louisiana State University Press, 1967), p. 16.
5. Adolph Gillis, *Ludwig Lewisohn: The Artist and His Message* (New York, 1933), p. 13.
6. Quoted by Gillis, p. 27.
7. Georg Hirschfeld, *The Mothers* (Garden City, N. Y.: Doubleday, Page,), p. xiii.
8. Ludwig Lewisohn, *The Spirit of Modern German Literature* (New York, 1916), p. 118.
9. Oscar Cargill, *Intellectual America* (New York, 1941), pp. 729-30.

10. Carl Van Doren, *Three Worlds*, (New York and London, 1936), p. 151.

11. H. L. Mencken, *The American Mercury* 10 (March, 1927):380.

12. Joseph Warren Beach, *The Outlook for American Prose* (Port Washington, N. Y., 1968), p. 215.

13. See Maurice Hindus, "Ludwig Lewisohn," pp. 24-25.

14. "*Up Stream* is a dynamic protest against the santification of a priestcraft in education, a revolt against the existence of an Anglo-Saxon intellectual aristocracy in a country that is the gathering together of a people from every corner of the earth" (*New York Times*, April 23, 1922, p. 22).

15. Stuart Pratt Sherman, *Americans* (New York, 1922), p. 24. Of the "modern" critics—Huneker, Mencken, Brooks, Hackett, Bourne, Lewisohn himself—Lewisohn anthologized in *A Modern Book of Criticism*, Sherman wrote: "restless impressionists, almost destitute of doctrine" (p. 22).

16. Burton Rascoe, *Before I Forget* (Garden City, N. Y.: Doubleday, Doran, 1937), pp. 339-401. See also William H. Nolte, *H. L. Mencken: Literary Critic* (Middletown, Conn.: Wesleyan University Press, 1966), pp. 172-75.

17. Jacob Zeitlin, "The Case of Mr. Lewisohn," *Menorah Journal* 8 (June, 1922):187.

18. Lionel Trilling, "Young in the Thirties," *Commentary* 41 (May, 1966):47.

19. See Abraham Chapman, introduction to *Jewish-American Literature: An Anthology* (New York and Scarborough, Ont.: New American Library, 1974, pp. xxix-xxx.

20. Ludwig Lewisohn, *Mid-Channel: An American Chronicle* (New York and London, 1929), p. 37.

21. Sisley Huddleston, *Paris Salons, Cafés, Studios* (New York: Blue Ribbon Books, 1928), pp. 252-53.

22. *New Yorker* 23 (March 29, 1947):110.

23. Joseph Wood Krutch, *More Lives Than One* (New York, 1962), p. 132.

24. Introduction to Lewisohn's *The Island Within* (Philadelphia, 1968), p. x.

25. Irwin Edman, *Nation* 128 (June 5, 1929):674.

26. Ludwig Lewisohn, *Haven* (New York, 1940), p. 43; hereafter page references cited in the text in this chapter.

27. Krutch, *More Lives*, p. 180.

28. Mark Schorer, *Sinclair Lewis: An American Life* (New York: McGraw-Hill, 1961), p. 279.

29. Sylvia Beach, *Shakespeare and Company* (Lincoln: University of Nebraska Press, 1980), p. 181.

30. E.g., Leslie Fiedler, *Waiting for the End* (New York: Dell, 1965), p. 77: "In fiction ... there were ... even quite serious novelists like Ben Hecht (before his removal to Hollywood) and Ludwig Lewisohn (before his surrender to Zionist apologetics)." Also Bernard Smith, *Forces in American Criticism* (New York, 1939), pp. 361-62.

31. James Elias Lewisohn, "My Father, Ludwig Lewisohn," *Midstream* 12 (Nov., 1966):48-52.

Chapter Two

1. Gerhart Hauptmann, *Dramatic Works*, vol. 3: *Domestic Dramas* (New York, 1914), p. vii.

2. Ludwig Lewisohn, *The Broken Snare* (New York, 1908), p. 3.

3. Ibid., p. 218.

4. Ludwig Lewisohn, *Mid-Channel* (New York and London, 1929), p. 71.

5. Ludwig Lewisohn, *Don Juan* (New York, 1923), pp. 9-10; hereafter cited in text as *DJ* followed by page number.

6. Henry Seidel Canby, review of *Don Juan* in *Nation* 117 (December 5, 1923):649.

7. Ludwig Lewisohn, *The Case of Mr. Crump* (New York, 1965), p. vii; hereafter cited in text as *CC* followed by page number.

8. Ludwig Lewisohn, *The Case of Mr. Crump* (Paris, 1926) p. 433.

9. Quoted from bookjacket, *The Case of Mr. Crump* (New York, 1965).

10. Ibid.

11. Joseph Wood Krutch, review of *The Case of Mr. Crump* in *Nation* 124 (February 9, 1927):149.

12. H. L. Mencken, review of *The Case of Mr. Crump* in *American Mercury* 10 (March, 1927):379.

13. Frederick J. Hoffman, *Freudianism and the Literary Mind* (New York, 1959), p. 282.

14. Ludwig Lewisohn, *Roman Summer* (New York and London, 1927), p. 7; hereafter cited in text as *RS* followed by page number.

15. Lionel Trilling, review of *Roman Summer* in *Menorah Journal* 14 (1928):108-9.

16. Ludwig Lewisohn, *Stephen Escott* (New York and London, 1930), p. 212.

17. Ibid.

18. Thyra Samter Winslow, review of *Stephen Escott* in *Book Review, New York Times* (April 20, 1930), p. 7.

19. Jonathan Daniels, review of *Stephen Escott* in *Saturday Review of Literature* 16 (March 15, 1930):821.

20. Hoffman, *Freudianism*, p. 76.

21. See Morris Cohen, *Reflections of a Wondering Jew* (New York, 1950), p. 123; also, Joseph Warren Beach, *The Outlook for American Prose* (Port Washington, N. Y., 1968), p. 216.

22. Ludwig Lewisohn, *The Golden Vase* (New York and London, 1931), p. 21.

23. Ibid., p. 37.

24. Ibid., p. 105.

25. Ludwig Lewisohn, *An Altar in the Fields* (New York, 1934), p. 39; hereafter cited in text as *AF* followed by page number.

26. Ludwig Lewisohn, *For Ever Wilt Thou Love* (New York, 1939), p. 192.

27. Lewisohn, *Haven* pp. 24-25.

28. Ludwig Lewisohn, *In a Summer Season* (New York, 1955), p. 213.

Chapter Three

1. Harold U. Ribalow, "Ludwig Lewisohn: 'The Island Within'," *Jewish Heritage* (Fall 1963), p. 48.

2. Ludwig Lewisohn, *The Island Within* (New York, 1940), p. 161; hereafter cited in text as *IW* followed by page number. All quotations are from the 1940 Modern Library edition.

3. Suicide as the culminating of one's sense of loss of racial identity appears as a theme in other works by Lewisohn. His first and only play, *Adam*, repeats this idea. The Worcester, Mass., *Telegram* summarizes the closet drama, written in 1929, as follows: "After the prologue come seven scenes dealing with the life of Adam, a Jewish boy who is so abused by the Christians that he runs away from home in a little German town on the Polish frontier. He goes to England and becomes a millionaire. He changes his name and marries an American girl.... But everywhere he finds himself an outcast, despised by the men who accept his money and aid. Even his wife feels a barrier between them, and leaves him, while he has separated himself from his fellow Jews." The hope-

lessness of his life leads to his suicide. The play was performed by an amateur group, the Knesset Israel alumni, on April 20, 1930. Lionel Trilling in the *New Republic* (April 9, 1930) thought the play bore stereotypes so dull Lewisohn would not have introduced them in narrative or exposition.

4. Bertrand Russell, review of *The Island Within* in *Nation* 132 (February 18, 1931):187.

5. Irwin Edman, review of *The Island Within* in *Menorah Journal* 14 (1928):511.

6. Bernard de Voto, review of *The Island Within* in *Saturday Review of Literature* 14 (May 5, 1928):840.

7. Joseph Smertenko, review of *The Island Within* in *Nation* 126 (April 18, 1928):482.

8. "Ludwig Lewisohn, who might have been expected to write a novel in the dominant mood of the early twenties, provided the counterbalance to Aiken by surprising a good many people with *The Island Within*. It was a distinctly new note, ethically speaking, in contemporary American fiction," wrote John Chamberlain, in "Drift and Mastery in our Novelists," *The Critique of Humanism*, ed. C. Hartley Grattan (New York, 1930), p. 268.

9. Ludwig Lewisohn, *The Last Days of Shylock* (New York, 1931), p. 4.

10. Ibid., p. 13.

11. Dated March 12, 1931. In the Lewisohn Archives at Brandeis University.

12. Granville Hicks, review of *The Last Days of Shylock* in *Nation* 132 (February 18, 1931):187.

13. Florence Haxton Britten, review of *The Last Days of Shylock* in *Books, New York Tribune*, January 11, 1931, p. 3.

14. Ludwig Lewisohn, "Writ of Divorcement," in *The Chosen*, ed. Harold U. Ribalow (London and New York: Abelard-Schuman, 1959), p. 140.

15. Ibid., p. 150.

16. John J. Smertenko, review of "Bolshevik" in *Opinion*, May 1933, p. 17.

17. Mary Ross, review of "By the Waters of Babylon" in *Books*, March 12, 1933, p. 3.

18. Lewisohn, *Haven*, p. 24.

19. Marianne Hauser, review of *Renegade* in *New York Times*, February 22, 1942, p. 7.

20. Ludwig Lewisohn, *Renegade* (New York, 1942), p. 53.

Chapter Four

1. Carl Van Doren, *Three Worlds*, pp. 147-48.

2. Alfred Kazin, *On Native Grounds* (New York: Doubleday, 1956), p. 206n.

3. Gerhart Hauptmann, *Dramatic Works*, vol. 2: *Social Dramas* (New York: B. W. Huebsch, 1913), p. ix.

4. Hauptmann, *Dramatic Works*, vol. 5: *Symbolic and Legendary Dramas* (New York, 1915), p. vii.

5. Hauptmann, *Dramatic Works*, vol. 1: *Social Dramas* (New York, 1912, p. xxxi.

6. Eric Bentley, *The Playwright as Thinker* (New York: Meridian, 1955), p. 261.

7. Adolph Gillis, *Ludwig Lewisohn: The Artist and his Message* (New York: Duffield and Green, 1933), pp. 33-34.

8. Ludwig Lewisohn, *The Modern Drama: An Essay in Interpretation* (New York, 1915), p. 13; hereafter cited in text as *Drama* followed by page number.

9. Ludwig Lewisohn, *The Spirit of Modern German Literature* (New York, 1916), p. 4, hereafter cited in text as *MGL* followed by page number.

10. Ludwig Lewisohn, *The Poets of Modern France* (New York, 1918), p. 1; hereafter cited in text as *Poets* followed by page number.

11. Ludwig Lewisohn, *A Modern Book of Criticism* (New York, 1919), p. 111.

12. Ibid., p. 178.

13. Kazin, *On Native Grounds* p. 206n.

14. Charles I. Glicksberg, ed., *American Literary Criticism, 1900-1950* (New York, 1952), p. 29.

15. Ludwig Lewisohn, "The Problem of Modern Poetry," *Bookman* 48 (1919):552.

16. Amy Lowell, "The Case of Modern Poetry versus Professor Lewisohn," *Bookman* 48 (1919):558.

17. Van Doren, pp. 146-47.

18. Joseph Wood Krutch, *Nation* 114 (April 26, 1922):500.

19. Barret H. Clark, *European Theories of the Drama* (New York: Crown, 1947), p. 517.

20. Ludwig Lewisohn, *The Drama and the Stage* (New York, 1922), p. 93; hereafter cited in text as *DS* followed by page number.

21. Ludwig Lewisohn, *The Creative Life* (New York, 1924), p. 14.

22. Ibid., p. 188.

23. Ludwig Lewisohn, *Cities and Men* (New York and London, 1927), p. 18; hereafter cited in text as *CM* followed by page number.

24. Charles Neider, ed., *The Stature of Thomas Mann* (New York: New Directions, 1947), p. 128.

Chapter Five

1. Ludwig Lewisohn, *The Story of American Literature* (New York, 1939), p. vii; hereafter cited in text as *SAL* followed by page number.

2. Louis Fraiberg, *Psychoanalysis and American Literary Criticism* (Detroit, 1960), pp. 120-60. Of Lewisohn, Fraiberg writes: "He apparently has a clearer grasp of psychoanalytic concepts than either Van Wyck Brooks in *The Ordeal of Mark Twain* or Joseph Wood Krutch in *Edgar Allan Poe*" (p. 156). But, Fraiberg continues, "He has not succeeded . . . in establishing a workable relationship between art and psychoanalysis" (p. 160).

3. Edgar Kemmler, in *The Irreverent Mr. Mencken* (Boston and Toronto: Wesleyan University Press, 1950), speaks of Lewisohn's chapter as a "full and inspired account of this battle" (p. 299n).

4. Otto Rank, *Art and Artist*, trans., C. F. Atkinson (New York: Alfred A. Knopf, 1952), pp. x-xi.

5. Ludwig Lewisohn, *The Magic Word: Studies in the Nature of Poetry* (New York, 1950), p. xiv; hereafter cited in text as *MW* followed by page number.

Chapter Six

1. Solomon Grayzel, *A History of the Contemporary Jews from 1900 to the Present* (New York: Atheneum, 1977), p. 97.

2. Stanley F. Chyet, "Lewisohn, a Zionist," *Rafael Mahler Jubilee Volume*, ed. Sh. Yeiven (Tel Aviv, 1974), p. 103.

3. Ibid., p. 106.

4. Edward Sapir, "Lewisohn's View of the Jewish Problem," *Menorah Journal* 12 (1926):215.

5. H. L. Mencken, review of *Mid-Channel* in *American Mercury* 17 (1929):80.

6. Ludwig Lewisohn, *Israel* (New York, 1925), p. 49; hereafter cited in text as *I* followed by page number.

7. Jacob Picard, *The Marked One and Twelve Other Stories* (Philadelphia: Jewish Publication Society, 1956), p. xv.

8. Sapir, in *Menorah Journal* 12 (1926):216.

9. I am in debt so far in this paragraph to Stanley F. Chyet, "Lewisohn, a Zionist." (See above.)

10. Ludwig Lewisohn, *The Permanent Horizon: A New Search for Old Truths* (New York, 1934), p. 15; hereafter cited in text as *PH* followed by page number.

11. Ernest Sutherland Bates, in "Lewisohn into Crump," *American Mercury* 31 (April, 1934): 450, attacks Lewisohn for abandoning the liberal position and having "the rules of the middle class established as the constitution of the universe." Certainly, Lewisohn's turn to neoconservatism must have struck many readers in the 1930s as unexpected.

12. Ludwig Lewisohn, *Rebirth: A Book of Modern Jewish Thought* (New York, 1935), p. xiv.

13. Ibid., p. xxxii.

14. Ibid., 274.

15. Ludwig Lewisohn, *The Answer* (New York, 1939), p. 340.

16. Ludwig Lewisohn, *The American Jew: Character and Destiny* (New York, 1950), pp. viii-ix.

17. Ibid., p. 31.

18. Samuel Caplan and Harold U. Ribalow, eds., *The Great Jewish Books* (New York: Washington Square Press, 1952), p. 15.

19. Ibid., p. 18.

20. Ludwig Lewisohn, ed. *Theodor Herzl: A Portrait for This Age* (Cleveland and New York: World, 1955), pp. 88-90.

21. Ibid., p. 90.

22. Ibid.

23. Ibid., p. 91.

Chapter Seven

1. C. Hugh Holman, *American Literary Scholarship*, ed. James Woodress (Durham, N. C.: Duke University Press, 1967), p. 179.

2. Robert E. Spiller *et al.*, eds., "Bibliography," *Literary History of the United States*, 4th ed., rev. (New York and London: Macmillan, 1974), 2: 612.

3. Geoffrey H. Hartman, *Criticism in the Wilderness: The Study of Literature Today* (New Haven: Yale University Press, 1980), p. 12.

4. H. L. Mencken, *American Mercury* 17 (1929): 379-80.

5. Leslie Fiedler, "The Jew in the American Novel," in *Collected Essays*, (New York, 1971) 2: 80.

6. Ibid., p. 81.

7. Bernard Sherman, *The Invention of the Jew* (New York: T. Yoseloff, 1969), p. 65.

8. Allen Guttman, *The Jewish Writer in America*, (New York: Oxford University Press, 1971), p. 106.

9. Howard M. Jones and Richard Ludwig, *Guide to American Literature* (Cambridge: Mass., Harvard University Press), p. 102.

10. Kazin, *On Native Grounds*, pp. 273-80.

11. Ibid., p. 275.

12. Ibid.

13. Ibid., 277.

14. Ibid., 273.

15. C. Hugh Holman, "The Defense of Art: Criticism Since 1930," in *The Development of American Literary Criticism,* ed. Floyd Stovall (Chapel Hill, N.C.: University of North Carolina Press, 1955), p. 219.

16. Jay B. Hubbell, *Who Are the Major American Writers?* (Durham, N.C.: Duke University Press, 1972), 256.

17. Carl Van Doren, *Three Worlds*, pp. 147-48.

18. Henri Peyre, *Failures of Criticism* (Ithaca, N.Y.: Cornell University Press, 1967) p. 83.

19. Marshall van Deusen, "Movements in Literary Criticism," in *American Literature Since 1900*, ed. Marcus Cunliffe (London: Barrie and Jenkins, 1975), p. 97.

20. Stuart P. Sherman, *Americans* (New York: Scribner's, 1922), pp. 21-22.

21. Vernon L. Parrington, *Main Currents in American Thought,* (New York: Harcourt, Brace, 1933) 3: 347.

22. Bernard Smith, *Forces in American Criticism* (New York: Harcourt Brace, 1939), p. 362.

23. Maxwell Geismar, *American Moderns* (New York: Hill and Wang, 1958), pp. 113-14.

Selected Bibliography

PRIMARY SOURCES

No complete list of Lewisohn's many literary efforts has been compiled. This bibliography lists his principal writings, categorized and in alphabetical order.

1. Autobiography

Haven (with Edna Manley Lewisohn). New York: Dial Press, 1940.
Mid-Channel: An American Chronicle. New York and London: Harper and Bros., 1929.
Up Stream: An American Chronicle. New York: Boni and Liveright, 1922.

2. Fiction

An Altar in the Fields. New York and London: Harper and Bros., 1934.
Annversary. New York: Farrar Straus and Co., 1948.
Breathe Upon These. Indianapolis: Bobbs-Merrill Co., 1944.
The Broken Snare. New York: B. W. Dodge, 1908.
The Case of Mr. Crump. Paris: Edward W. Titus, 1926.
Don Juan. New York: Boni and Liveright, 1923.
For Ever Wilt Thou Love. New York: Dial Press, 1939.
The Golden Vase. New York and London: Harper and Bros., 1931.
In a Summer Season. New York: Farrar Straus and Co., 1955.
The Island Within. New York and London: Harper and Bros., 1928.
The Last Days of Shylock. New York and London: Harper and Bros., 1931.
Renegade. New York: Dial Press, 1942.
Roman Summer. New York and London: Harper and Bros., 1927.
Stephen Escott. New York and London: Harper and Bros., 1930.
This People. New York and London: Harper and Bros., 1933.
   (Novellas.)
Trumpet of Jubilee. New York and London: Harper and Bros., 1937.

3. Drama

Adam: a dramatic history. New York and London: Harper and Bros.,
   1929.

4. Criticism

Cities and Men. New York and London: Harper and Bros., 1927.
The Creative Life. New York: Boni and Liveright, 1924.
Expression in America. New York and London: Harper and Bros., 1932.
   (Reprinted as *The Story of American Literature.* New York:
   Random House, 1939, with a new postscript.)
The Drama and the Stage. New York: Harcourt Brace and Co., 1922.
The Magic Word: Studies in the Nature of Poetry. New York:
   Farrar Straus and Co., 1950.
The Modern Drama: An Essay in Interpretation. New York: B. W.
   Huebsch, 1915.
The Poets of Modern France. New York: B. W. Huebsch, 1918. (With
   translations by Lewisohn.)
The Spirit of Modern German Literature. New York: B. W. Huebsch,
   1916.

5. Polemics

The American Jew: Character and Destiny. New York: Farrar Straus
   and Co., 1950.
The Answer. New York: Liveright, 1939
Israel. New York: Boni and Liveright, 1925.
The Permanent Horizon: A New Search for Old Truths. New York:
 ·   Harper and Bros., 1934.
"What Is This Jewish Heritage?" New York: B'nai Brith Hillel Founda-
   tion, 1954. (Pamphlet.)

6. Anthologies And Collections: Editor

Among The Nations: Three Tales and a Play about Jews. New York:
   Farrar Straus and Co., 1948.
Creative America. New York and London: Harper and Bros., 1933.
German Style: An Introduction to the Study of German Prose. New
   York: Henry Holt and Co., 1910. (Text.)

Goethe: The Story of a Man. 2 vols. New York: Farrar Straus, and Co., 1949. Selections from Goethe to illustrate his life; translated by the editor.

Jewish Short Stories. New York: Behrman House, 1945

A Modern Book of Criticism. New York: Boni and Liveright, 1919.

Rebirth: A Book of Modern Jewish Thought. New York and London: Harper and Bros., 1935.

Theodor Herzl: A Portrait for this Age. New York and Cleveland: World, 1955.

7. Chief Translations Into English

Bartsch, Rudolph Hans. *Elizabeth Koett.* New York: D. Fitzgerald, 1910.

Sundermann, Hermann. *The Indian Lily.* New York: B. W. Huebsch, 1911.

Hauptmann, Gerhart. *Dramatic Works.* 7 vols. New York: R. W. Huebsch, 1912-1917.

Pinski, David. *The Treasure.* New York: B. W. Huebsch, 1915.

Hirschfeld, Georg. *The Mothers.* Garden City: Doubleday, Page, 1916.

Lattzko, Andreas. *The Judgment of Peace.* New York: Boni and Liveright, 1919.

Wasserman, Jacob. *The World's Illusion:* Harcourt, 1920.

Wasserman, Jacob. *Wedlock.* New York: Boni and Liveright, 1926.

Guttman, Bernhard. *Ambition.* New York: Harper and Bros., 1931.

Werfel, Franz. *The Eternal Road.* New York: The Viking Press, 1936.

Rilke, Rainer Maria. *Thirty-one Poems.* New York: B. Ackerman, 1946.

Buber, Martin, *For the Sake of Heaven.* Philadelphia: Jewish Publication Society, 1945.

Morgenstern, Soma. *In My Father's Pastures.* Philadelphia: Jewish Publication Society, 1947.

Brod, Max. *Unambo.* Philadelphia: Jewish Publication Society, 1952.

Picard, Jacob. *The Marked One and Twelve Other Stories.* Philadelphia: Jewish Publication Society, 1956.

SELECTED SECONDARY SOURCES

Some of the best comments on Lewisohn are in book reviews; these are so indicated. Only one full-length study (1933), by Adolph Gillis, has been published.

Analyticus [James Waterman Wise.] *Jews are Like That!* New York: Brentano's, 1928, pp. 109-26.

Bates, Ernest Sutherland. "Lewisohn Into Crump," *American Mercury* 31 (April, 1934): 441-50. Laments Lewisohn's abandoning of his earlier liberalism; written with sting.

Beach, Joseph Warren. *The Outlook for American Prose.* 1926. reprint. Port Washington, N.Y.: Kennikat Press, 1968, pp. 214-16.

Bragman, Louis J. "The Case of Ludwig Lewisohn." *American Journal of Psychiatry* 11 (Sept. 1931): 319-31. Enlightening psychological approach to Lewisohn, marred by several sentences damaging to its credibility.

Brande, Dorothea. "Mr. Lewisohn Interprets America." *American Review* 2 (1933): 189-98. Attacks Lewisohn as an "alien" unqualified to assess "our" literature; combines some critical acumen with much prejudice.

Cargill, Oscar. *Intellectual America: Ideas on the March.* New York: Macmillan, 1941.

Chamberlain, John. "Drift and Morality in Our Novelists" in *The Critique of Humanism,* ed. C. Hartley Grattan, New York: Brewer and Warren, 1930, pp. 257-80. Assesses *The Island Within* favorably among other novels. This *New York Times* book critic generally gave Lewisohn sympathetic reviews.

Chyet, Stanley F. "Lewisohn, a Zionist." *Rafael Mahler Jubilee Volume,* ed. Sh. Yeiven. Tel Aviv: Vered Press, 1974, pp. 103-36. Thorough discussion of subject; best account thus far.

_____."Lewisohn and Crévecoeur." *Chicago Jewish Forum* 22 (Winter 1973-74): pp. 130-36.

_____."Ludwig Lewisohn in Charleston (1892-1903)." *American Jewish Historical Society* 50 (March, 1965): 296-322. Chyet's three articles contain biographical information on Lewisohn's early years.

_____. "Ludwig Lewisohn: The Years of Becoming." *American Jewish Archives* 11 (October, 1959): 125-47.

Collins, Joseph. *Taking the Literary Pulse: Psychological Studies of Life and Letters.* New York: George H. Doran Co., 1924. Includes a venemous attack on *Don Juan*: "I do not know that 'Don Juan' is at all autobiographical, but Lucien Curtis reminds me of the man who went upstream so successfully, despite the hydra-headed, anti-semitic monster who tried to devour him."

Eckerling, David. "The Case of Ludwig Lewisohn." *Reflex* 5 (September, 1929): 14-20. Interprets Lewisohn's turn from objective critic to subjective novelist as a change for the worse; employs the popular designation for Lewisohn as a "case."

Edman, Irwin. Review of *The Island Within*. *Menorah Journal* 14 (1928): 508-11. Well-written appreciation, indicative of impression novel made on many Jewish intellectuals.

Fiedler, Leslie A. "The Jew in the American Novel." *Collected Essays*, vol. 2. New York: Stein and Day, 1971. Condescending comments, similar to others recorded in Fiedler's essays: "There is a real pathos in the efforts of the Jewish intellectual to see himself as Don Juan, an essential vanity of his striving to embody current themes of sexual freedom." Lewisohn deserves better than being analyzed like a butterfly on a pin.

Foerster, Norman. *Toward Standards*. New York: Farrar and Rinehart, 1930. A Humanist attacks Lewisohn and other Moderns for "Impressionism."

Fraiberg, Louis. *Psychoanalysis and American Literary Criticism*. Detroit: Wayne State University Press, 1960. See especially chapter 7, "Ludwig Lewisohn and the Puritan Inhibitions of American Literature." Of Lewisohn as Freudian critic in *Expression in America*, Fraiberg sees him as a symptomatic early failure; Hoffman is more commendatory; Walter Sutton's is a balanced discussion (see below).

Gillis, Adolph. *Ludwig Lewisohn: The Artist and His Message*. New York: Duffield and Green, 1933. Adulatory in tone, but informative.

Hartman, Geoffrey H. *Criticism in the Wilderness: The Study of Literature Today*. New Haven: Yale University Press, 1980.

Hindus, Maurice. "Ludwig Lewisohn: From Assimilation to Zionism." *Jewish Frontier* 31 (February 1964): 20-30. Best recent appreciation.

Hoffman, Frederic J. *Freudianism and the Literary Mind*. New York: Grove Press, 1959. Favorable assessment of Lewisohn as a crusader against sexual repression and a torchbearer of Freud.

Hubbell, Jay B. *Who Are the Major American Writers?* Durham, N.C.: Duke University Press, 1972, pp. 256-57. Balanced assessment of *Expression of America*.

Kazin, Alfred. *On Native Grounds*. New York: Doubleday, 1956. Mingles perceptive comments on Lewisohn's criticism with strictures against Lewisohn as "frenzied apostle."

Krutch, Joseph Wood. More Lives Than One. New York: William Sloane Associates, 1962. A memoir, with some reminiscences of Lewisohn.

──────────. Review of *The Case of Mr. Crump. The Nation* 124 (February 9, 1927): 149. Uneasily appreciative review. Krutch, Lewisohn's successor as drama critic for the *Nation*, like Carl Van Doren, literary editor during Lewisohn's regime, was a friend and a favorable critic.

Lewisohn, James Elias. "My Father, Ludwig Lewisohn." *Midstream* 12 (November, 1966): 48-52. Important as biography; evidence of a somewhat troubled relationship.

Lowell, Amy. "The Case of Modern Poetry versus Professor Lewisohn." *Bookman* 48 (1919): 558-66. Able rebuttal of Lewisohn's case against modern poetry in the same issue, pp. 549–57.

Mencken, H. L. Review of *The Case of Mr. Crump. American Mercury* 10 (March, 1927): 380. An appreciative, beautifully written appraisal.

──────────. Review of *Mid-Channel. American Mercury* 17 (1929): 379-80. Thoughtful assessment.

Millett, Fred, ed. *Contemporary American Authors.* New York: Harcourt Brace and Co., 1940. Useful biographical sketch and bibliography.

Okin, Leslie. "The Dramatic Criticism of Ludwig Lewisohn: A Critical Study." 2 vols. Doctoral thesis, New York University, 1977. Close examination of Lewisohn as drama critic for the *Nation*, 1919–1924.

Ribalow, Harold U. "Ludwig Lewisohn's 'The Island Within'." *Jewish Heritage* (Fall, 1963), pp. 44-48. The novel in retrospect, seen as significant today.

Sapir, Edward. "Lewisohn's View of the Jewish Problem." *Menorah Journal* 12 (1926): 214-18. Review of *Israel*. Admits bias against premises of the book, but subjects it to thorough analysis.

Shafer, Robert. *Paul Elmer More and American Criticism,* New Haven: Yale University Press, 1936. Includes More's sustained attack on Lewisohn, especially on the Freudian aspects of *Expression in America*, pp. 40-50; also, in appendices, attacks on More by Lewisohn, Boyd, Hackett, Mencken, and Edmund Wilson.

Sherman, Stuart Pratt. *Americans.* New York: Charles Scribner's Sons, 1922, pp. 20-25. A Humanist's attack upon the younger critics, including Lewisohn, whom he calls a "group of shivering young

Davids" facing an "army of Goliaths." Sherman refers to them as "alien-minded critics." He especially disliked *A Modern Book of Criticism.*

Singer, David F. "Ludwig Lewisohn: A Paradigm of American Jewish Return." *Judaism* 14 (1965): 319-29. A good study of Lewisohn's return to Judaism as seen in his writings.

Smith, Bernard. *Forces in American Criticism.* New York: Harcourt Brace and Co., 1939. A Marxist critic's antagonism toward *Expression in America.* Of Lewisohn's *Nation* days, Smith writes: " ... it is plain that Lewisohn's misty and emotional philosophizing reflected a wholly unscientific, a non-materialist, conception of the history of society."

Sutton, Walter. *Modern American Criticism.* Englewood Cliffs, N.J.: Prentice-Hall, 1963. Chapter 2, "Early Psychological Criticism," examines *Expression in America, inter alia.*

Van Doren, Carl. *Three Worlds.* New York and London: Harper and Bros., 1936. Thoughful and sympathetic comments, well-written.

Zeitlin, Jacob. "The Case of Mr. Lewisohn." *Menorah Journal* 8 (June, 1922): 1187-91. Review of *Up Stream.* More moderate than Sherman, Zeitlin charges Lewisohn with exaggeration but extends some appreciation.

Index